Rudiments of Faith

Daily Readings for Living on a Spiritual Basis

Rev Dr Chris Noble

Published by New Generation Publishing in 2022

Copyright © Rev Dr Chris Noble 2022

First Edition

The author asserts the moral right under the Copyright, Designs and Patents Act 1988 to be identified as the author of this work.

All Rights reserved. No part of this publication may be reproduced, stored in a retrieval system or transmitted, in any form or by any means without the prior consent of the author, nor be otherwise circulated in any form of binding or cover other than that which it is published and without a similar condition being imposed on the subsequent purchaser.

Except for the author's own translation, the scripture quotations in this book have been sourced from the following translations of the Holy Bible. King James Version. Crown copyright. The New King James Version. Copyright 1982 by Thomas Nelson, Inc. Used by permission. All rights reserved. New International Version®, NIV®. Copyright © 1973, 1978, 1984, 2011 by Biblica, Inc.™ Used by permission of Zondervan. All rights reserved worldwide. The "NIV" and "New International Version" are trademarks registered in the United States Patent and Trademark Office by Biblica, Inc.™ The Good News Bible ®1994 published by the Bible Societies/Harper Collins Publishers Ltd UK. Used with permission. The Message. Copyright ©1993, 2002, 2018 by Eugene H. Peterson. Used by permission of NavPress. All rights reserved. English Standard Version (ESV) copyright © 2001 by Crossway, a publishing ministry of Good News Publishers. All rights reserved.

ISBN
    Paperback   978-1-80369-614-0
    eBook   978-1-80369-615-7

www.newgeneration-publishing.com

Introduction

At the age of eleven, my cousin who was a professional drummer, gave me a practice pad, a pair of drumsticks and a book of rudiments. Each day I practised the short rudimentary exercises in that book and almost without realising it, I learned to play the drums.

These meditations and prayers are the rudiments of faith that I practice every day for the realisation and development of my inner life with God and my ongoing personal discovery of the presence of his Spirit within me.

A deeper inner life with God and the conscious contact with him that it brings are subtle things but with practice, we can come to realise a personal and spiritual connection that we never thought possible.

I have written these meditations in the first person because they come from my own lived experience of faith. I offer them as a springboard and a catalyst for developing and deepening your relationship with God along with an ever-increasing awareness of the movement of his Spirit in your life.

To get the most from these spiritual exercises, I would suggest that you start your day by setting aside a few minutes to read and reflect on the rudiment for the day.

In time you may want to linger with the Lord and use these rudiments as an introduction to a longer and deeper time of meditation and prayer.

Dedication

Dedicated To Deborah
My Faithful & Noble Wife.
Proverbs 31.10-11.

January

1st Spiritual Awakening

Change and become like little children.
Matthew 18.3

It is only as I have let go of much of my so-called knowledge that religious information has been replaced by a real and deepening relationship with God the Father, the Son and the Holy Spirit.

This has come to me as I have begun to realise my relationship as a child of God in a loving heavenly family who are actively involved in my life and want the best for me.

Spiritual awakening is not just a matter of religious knowledge. True knowledge of God is relational.

Prayer: God, draw me deeper into my relationship with you.

2nd Spiritual Transformation

Transformed into his likeness.
2 Corinthians 3.18

Religious knowledge will follow faith but true spiritual growth is about being transformed through relationship and fellowship with God.

It is in this relationship that the inner work of transformation by the Spirit takes place and it is through this vital connection that true spiritual growth happens.

Through my experience of this relationship, God has been changing me from the inside out as my heart is being renewed and transformed by his life-giving Spirit.

Prayer: God, I consent to your Spirit's work within me.

3rd Spiritual Illumination

God made his light shine in our hearts.
2 Corinthians 4.6

Spiritual enlightenment comes as God shines his light and brings his life into our spirit and soul.

As God shines the light of his presence into my spirit, my spiritual senses come alive to him and his relationship with me is expanded and increased.

As God draws close his light is increased inside my spirit and soul. It is this spiritual illumination that changes the way I see and experience everything, including myself.

Prayer: Holy Spirit, illuminate my life with your presence.

4th God Inside

It pleased God to reveal his Son in me.
Galatians 1.16

Christ lives in me. He reveals himself and makes his presence known within. His habitation within is the centre of my life and without his inner presence, I have nothing.

No longer does my life revolve around my self-life, instead it centres on God, who by his Spirit has taken up residence in my spirit.

His presence within me is the foundation upon which my life is constructed. His presence flows from within and gives life to me and to everyone he touches through me.

Prayer: Holy Spirit, reveal yourself in me and through me.

5th Removing the Veil

The veil is taken away.
2 Corinthians 3.16

Having spiritual truth is not the same as knowing it in my inner self.

Just because I read words about the freedom that God offers me doesn't mean that it has been activated within me.

Spiritual enlightenment requires the removal of the veil so that the light of God can get through.

When God removed the veil, I began to see, hear, and feel his presence as the eyes of my heart were no longer covered over and my spiritual senses were activated.

Prayer: God, activate my spiritual senses.

6th God is Active

God is living and active.
Hebrews 4.12

God is not dead he is very much alive. He is so much more involved in our lives and our world than we know or think.

He is living and active which means that he is doing all sorts of things around us in miraculous ways that are far beyond our understanding or perception.

I am asking him to continue to open my spiritual eyes so that I can see what he is doing.

Instead of missing or dismissing the movements of God, I am paying attention and seeking to perceive the things that he is doing all around me.

Prayer: God, open my eyes to see you at work.

7th Spiritual Thirst

My soul thirsts for the living God.
Psalm 42.2

My heart's cry is that I may know God more and more in my life.

I am hungry and thirsty for God.

I long for more of his loving presence within me.

I am praying that God will continue to open the eyes of my heart so that I may see him more clearly and love him more dearly.

I want to know him more than I have ever known him before.

Prayer: God, I hunger and thirst for you.

8th Living in Him

In him, we live and move and have our being.
Acts 17.28

I am seeking to live in the truth and reality that every move I make, every step I take, and every breath I breathe, is in him.

In him, I live and move and have my being. I am in Christ and Christ is in me.

I am no longer living independently of God. Instead, I am seeking to live and move in total dependence on him.

Prayer: Jesus, may I live, move, and be in you, as you are in me.

9th The Way Back to God

Separation to the Lord.
Numbers 6.2

My way back to fellowship with God has come through separation from my ego. My ego is constantly trying to find ways of expanding itself and separating me from God.

It is only by learning to surrender to the power of God that the grip of my ego is released and its power over me is broken.

This is where the battle for control of my life has raged as my ego-driven soul power has come face to face with the power of God's Spirit living within.

As I surrender to the power and presence of God in my spirit, I find myself being separated from the domination of my ego and set free to live for him.

Prayer: Lord, break me free from the control of my ego.

10th Trusting God

Look at the birds of the air.
Matthew 6.26

My ego believed that life couldn't take care of itself without me managing it in some way.

Ungoverned, my ego did not believe that life would unfold the way it was supposed to without the imposition of my will.

My ego could not trust God to provide. It was worried about not having enough and always seemed to want more.

I am counselling my ego to look at the birds of the air who neither sow nor reap, yet my heavenly Father cares for them all.

Prayer: Lord, help me to trust you in all things, both great and small.

11th Guarding My Heart

Above all else, guard your heart.
Proverbs 4.23

I am focussing on guarding my heart against attacks of fear, anxiety, worry and doubt.

Faith comes by hearing but the other side of the coin is that fear, anxiety, worry and doubt also come by that route.

When it comes to hearing and listening, I need to be careful about who and what I listen to.

I need to guard the gates of my heart so that I don't welcome unwanted visitors such as fear, anxiety, worry or doubt.

Prayer: Lord, guard my heart against fear, worry, anxiety and doubt.

12th Heavenly Mindset

Set your minds on things above.
Colossians 3.2

My self-centred ego has not been the only barrier between me and my God.

The materialistic focus of the world around me is continually calling for my attention and seeking to draw me out from the realm of the Spirit.

There is a battle for my mind and my attention. It's always a good day when I've got my mind set on things above.

Prayer: Holy Spirit, keep my heart and mind set on things above.

13th Self-Reliance

This happened that we might not rely on ourselves.
2 Corinthians 1.9

As I sit down to be still before my creator, I am conscious that by myself I can't connect. I am reminded that I need God to come to me as I present myself to him.

My spiritual books and prompts are but tools in the hands of the master. As I sit quietly and start to engage with their themes, I am reaching out beyond them in my spirit. I am questing for his presence.

I am reminded that in the realm of the Spirit self-reliance doesn't work.

Prayer: Lord, I am relying on you and your presence in my life.

14th Spiritual Not Religious

What has happened to all your joy?
Galatians 4.15

Any spirituality that delivers real spiritual life has to contend with the giant of religion. Religious systems with their impressive performances, buildings, ascetic practices and many other outward expressions can cast a heavy shadow over a joyful expression of true faith.

Religious traditions that appeal merely to my natural soul-life can never deliver the freedom, joy and fullness of Spirit that God wants me to have.

Prayer: Holy Spirit, develop my internal atmosphere of joy.

15th Trusting the Plan

I know the plans I have for you.
Jeremiah 29.11

I know that God has the plan and the blueprint for my life. I believe that his plan is the best one and the only one that will fulfil my destiny in this world.

This also means that my fears and anxiety about today, tomorrow and my whole future are all built on a basic lack of trust in God's plan and his good purposes for my life.

Prayer: Lord, I choose to trust the plans you have for me.

16th Spiritual Formation

Until Christ be formed in you.
Galatians 4.19

The internal and external conflict that I experience as I seek the enlargement of my spiritual life reveals a deep-seated resistance to spiritual growth from within my old self-life.

The formation of the life and character of Christ within me is something that I deeply desire but also resist.

It pleases God to reveal his Son in me and it's a glorious thing, but this comes through travail as day by day my soul surrenders itself to the control of God's Spirit.

Prayer: Lord, may the character of Christ be formed within my heart.

17th Spiritual Maturity

Conformed to the likeness of his Son.
Romans 8.29

Whilst it is important to grow up in our knowledge of the truth, spiritual maturity is not confined to the acquisition of more knowledge.

Through the impetus of God's Spirit within I find myself growing in a more mature faith as my life is in being conformed to the image of God's Son.

Over time I can see progress as I am being transformed in my inner being so that the image of Christ, however opaque, is visible.

This is not to claim perfection but I can see progress as I look back and see how I used to be.

Prayer: Lord, conform me into the likeness of your Son.

18th So Afraid

Why are you so afraid, do you still have no faith?
Mark 4.40

At the root of fear is self-reliance.

My fear level has all too often been an indicator of my lack of faith and trust in God. This seems like a tough diagnosis but that's the reality of it.

If I am relying on myself and my own resources then fear inevitably creeps in. When I turn my life situation over to God then serenity comes.

Prayer: Lord, take my fear and replace it with faith in you.

19th Calm Down

Quiet! Be still!
Mark 4.39

These words of command were spoken in a situation of great jeopardy. There was a huge amount of fear in the hearts of the people who heard them.

They had been unexpectedly hit by a furious squall that sent them into panic mode. The situation just got worse and they were deeply afraid of the outcome.

God seemed to be unconcerned and they were beside themselves with fear, but when they remembered that God was with them, the situation changed immediately.

Faith began to replace fear and God brought his peace. They calmed down and got on with their journey.

Prayer: Lord, replace my fears with your peace.

20th Spiritual Enlargement

I am again in travail.
Galatian 4.19

As my life moves increasingly onto a spiritual basis, I have to face the frustrations and difficulties that come with the quest for spiritual enlargement.

Spiritual growth is fraught with opposition as my desire for spiritual progress takes me into the realms of spiritual conflict.

There is the internal battle with the ego that doesn't like giving up control, as well as external forces that arise to stand in the way of my spiritual progress.

Prayer: Lord, bring me through the barriers to spiritual growth.

21st Your Will

Your will be done.
Matthew 6.10

Anxiety flows into me if I choose to take my will back. Stress comes into my spirit, as does fear.

Fear that I won't get what I want. Fear that things won't go my way or fear that I will lose something that I already have.

Worry returns when I take my will back because if I am back in charge of my life then it's all down to me again

I need to let God be God. He is the one who has to be ruling and reigning in my life.

Prayer: Lord, your will not my will be done.

22nd The Spirit of Life

The Spirit of Life.
Romans 8.2

Deep down my soul loves God but it tends to want God on its terms.

My soul wants to be in control of the learning and it tries to apply truth to itself rather than responding to the Spirit of life that is rising up from within.

Life-giving spiritual learning takes place when I allow the Spirit of life in Jesus to rise up within me.

Prayer: Spirit of Jesus rise up within me and give me life.

23rd I Want to See

I want to see.
Mark 10.51

Physical sight is a most valuable thing but spiritual sight is even more precious. Spiritual blindness is not as obvious as physical blindness which is why it was not until my spiritual eyes were opened that I realised how blind I had been.

The prophets of old spoke of a people who walked in darkness without the illumination of the Spirit. Without the light of God's Spirit in my heart that is what I am like.

The gift of spiritual seeing came to people who were desperate for the Lord to open their eyes. It is the same today with spiritual sight as it is not given to the casual seeker.

It costs me to see. I have to want it and go after it.

Prayer: Lord, I want to see.

24th Recovery of Sight

Let me recover my sight.
Luke 18.41

Spiritual seeing is a gift which if neglected or dismissed, can be lost. Spiritual sight needs to be cultivated and developed as it is not a static thing.

There are always new things to see and new discoveries to be made in the realm of the Spirit. I need God's Spirit of revelation to open up for me the things that he wants me to see.

Even if I sense that I am losing my spiritual vision or that my vision is being impaired, it is never too late for me to seek recovery of my spiritual sight.

Prayer: Lord, let me recover my sight.

25th Living Epistles

Tablets of the Human Heart.
2 Corinthians 3.3

The presence of the Spirit of God in my heart reflects the glory of God in ever-increasing measure.

Unveiled, our hearts are like mirrors that reflect the light of God's glorious presence in the world around us.

We are living epistles. Letters, not written with ink on paper, but permanently marked with the Spirit of God as his reflected glory leaves its indelible impression on the tablets of our human hearts.

Prayer: Lord, mark the tablet of my human heart with your image.

26th Known in Heaven

Rejoice because your names are written in heaven.
Luke 10.20

To be recognised, to make a name for ourselves, or to gain some form of status is the great obsession of our age.

Celebrities are venerated as were the saints of old, but what about me? Who is going to notice me? What if I never make a name for myself? What if I die in obscurity and leave no visible or lasting trace of my time on the earth?

The answer that Jesus gives is wonderfully liberating. He says that the place where I need to be recognised is in heaven and that is where my name needs to be known.

Prayer: Lord, remember me when I am ignored or forgotten here on earth.

27th Set Apart from Birth

God, who set me apart from birth.
Galatians 1.15

With growing awareness of the enlightenment that I am receiving through the action of God's Spirit within, comes a sense of my eternal destiny as I realise that God has had his hand on me from before my birth.

I have come to realise what I already knew deep down inside which is that I have all along been foreknown and set apart for God.

Our lives are not just meaningless accidents. We are known, wanted and loved, having been chosen before the foundation of the world.

Prayer: Lord, thank you that I am known, wanted, and loved.

28th Beginning to See

I see men like trees walking.
Mark 8.24

It is a wonderful thing to have a spiritual awakening and to start to see in the Spirit. For me, it was a profound experience and the beginning of a journey into a new order of life with the Spirit of God within.

As we start to walk in the light we begin to see with the eyes of our hearts. With the acquisition of these new spiritual lenses, what was previously blurred or misty comes into focus for the first time.

My awakening was just the beginning of the development of my spiritual sight and senses which have been activated by the Spirit of God living within.

Prayer: Lord, thank you for my spiritual awakening and the gift of spiritual sight.

29th Seeing Things

Things in heaven and on earth.
Ephesians 1.10

My spiritual sight has been a wonderful gift as I have been able to learn to perceive some of the heavenly realities that are all around me.

I notice things and see things that previously would have gone unnoticed or unrecognised.

I have become aware of my spiritual radar picking up the previously hidden and unseen movements of the Spirit of God.

God shows me things that I never knew or saw until my eyes were opened.

Prayer: Lord, increase my vision for your heavenly realities here on earth.

30th Surrender

No one can say, 'Jesus is Lord,' except by the Holy Spirit.
1 Corinthians 12.3

It is only through the power of the indwelling Spirit that I am set free from my self-life and enabled to live under the Lordship of Jesus Christ.

I can't do this with my unaided willpower.

He takes his rightful place as I surrender control of my will, my mind and my life to him.

Prayer: Lord, help me to surrender my self-life to you.

31st The Counsel of God

He will give you another counsellor.
John 14.16

Our Lord showed what it means to live in fellowship with the Father and the Holy Spirit. He was constantly seeking their guidance and direction at every turn of the day.

Living in Christ means that the counsellor is now within me, and if I am able, willing, and available to listen, he will direct my path.

I am no longer self-propelled, but God-directed, as I learn to tune in to his movements and spiritual direction within me.

Prayer: Lord, teach me to hear and to follow your counsel.

February

1st The Promised Land

By faith, he made his home in the promised land.
Hebrews 11.9

The promised land is no longer a physical territory but a spiritual one and as with the promised land of old, I have territory within my heart that is still not surrendered to the Lord.

My self-life barricades itself into strongholds in my soul. These are the fortified cities in the promised land of my inner self.

My ego makes its stand from these citadels of self as it wages war against the advancing Christ-life within.

This continual advance of the life of Jesus within me gradually weakens and erodes these bastions of self until they finally give way.

In this way, Jesus gains further territory in the promised land of my soul.

Prayer: Lord, please take control over my strongholds of resistance to you.

2nd The Fullness of God

Filled with all the fullness of God.
Ephesians 3.19

Spiritual hunger is a good thing but it is also true that there will be fullness. Indeed, our Lord instructed us that the blessing of spiritual hunger is in the promise that we shall be filled.

Fullness is something to be sought after. We are encouraged to be filled with all the fullness of God.

Jesus expands his presence and rule within me as I come to him with my spiritual hunger.

Prayer: God, fill me with all your fullness.

3rd The Great Exception

Except by the Holy Spirit.
1 Corinthians 12.3

No one can say 'Jesus is Lord' except by the Holy Spirit. Of course, people can say this but for it to be a reality, and to be able to mean it, is a different matter altogether.

It is only by the action of the Holy Spirit in my heart that I can arrive at a place in my life where Jesus is Lord. Where he is 100% in charge of my life.

The flesh, that is the carnal nature, cannot do this. It is only the presence of Jesus Christ by his Spirit in my heart that can bring me to this place of total surrender to his governance.

Prayer: Lord Jesus, help me to surrender to your governance in every aspect of my life.

4th The Worship of the Heart

Sing and make music in your heart to the Lord.
Ephesians 5.19

The presence of Jesus in my heart is evidenced by the Spirit of worship that spontaneously wells up within me at all hours of the day and night, often when I least expect it.

Like an internal fountain of life, I find that praise and adoration for Jesus rise up from within my spirit.

Sometimes I experience this with words or songs but often it is just the silent worship of my heart that is being expressed internally in my spirit.

Prayer: Lord, increase your Spirit of worship in my heart.

5th Increasing Glory

Transformed into his likeness with ever-increasing glory.
2 Corinthians 3.18

The Spirit of the Lord is manifested in my life as my heart is being changed and transformed into his likeness with ever-increasing glory.

This transformation comes from the activity of the Spirit of the Lord who is at work within my heart.

Rather than fading away or becoming dull over time the radiance of the Lord in my heart is increasing as more and more space is being freed up for him.

Prayer: Thank you Holy Spirit for your ever-increasing life in my heart.

6th The Sacred Gaze

Gazing at the radiance.
2 Corinthians 3.13

Reading about someone else's experience of the Lord is not the same as experiencing it for myself.

I can read, write or even speak about the things that the Lord promises but that is not the same as experiencing and appropriating them for myself.

My gaze only becomes truly sacred when I am seeing what I am talking about.

Prayer: Lord, help me to see and to know what I am talking about.

7th Soul Power

That we might not rely on ourselves but on God.
2 Corinthians 1.9

Soul power is a very potent and deceptive force that I have to watch like a hawk. The latent power of my soul can be very dangerous and destructive to my life in the Spirit.

My soul power is my own latent spiritual capability that is independent of the Lord. It is the part of me that wants to run my own spiritual life my own way without God.

Instead of seeking to live for God the way he wants me to, my soul power seeks to do it my way. It is a spiritual manifestation of my ego.

It is a trickster that will try to convince me to do spiritual work in the power of my soul and flesh instead of relying on the Holy Spirit.

Prayer: Lord, help me to rely on you and not on my soul-power.

8th Spiritual Growth

Transformed into his likeness.
2 Corinthians 3.18

Spiritual growth for me is about being transformed and conformed to the image of God's Son. It is a steady progression and a consistent movement towards this end.

Spiritual growth that leads me to maturity is to be recognised in my conformity to the image of Jesus.

He is my yardstick and the measure of my progress. It is against his life and his life only that my life is to be judged.

Prayer: Lord, conform me to the image of your Son.

9th Spiritual Birth

Flesh gives birth to flesh but Spirit gives birth to Spirit.
John 3.6

True spiritual life comes only from the Spirit of the Lord. The Natural life of the flesh can create natural life but not spiritual life.

When my flesh tries to create spiritual life, it just creates religion, but when I get out of the way and let the Spirit of the Lord give birth to Spirit, then I experience real spiritual life.

Prayer: Holy Spirit, continue to give birth to fresh life in my spirit.

10th Living from Within

The Kingdom of God is within you.
Luke 17.21

Underneath my external existence, I have a secret life with God. Through the regenerative power of God's Spirit within me, I experience a powerful inner life with him.

The extent to which I welcome and make room for Jesus in my heart is the determining factor in the intensity of his presence within me.

The Kingdom, which is the government of God in my life, flows from the unfettered life of Christ within.

Prayer: Lord, I give you permission to expand your territory in my heart.

11th Tomorrow's World

You do not know what tomorrow will bring.
James 4.14

I find myself wanting to control the future but the reality is that I have far less control than I would like to think that I have.

In my natural self-life, I want to trust in myself rather than in God. For me letting go and letting God is far harder than it sounds.

This is where the rubber hits the road in terms of my trust in God. This is where my faith becomes real as I let go of my will and actively trust God with my future.

Prayer: Lord, help me to actively trust you with my future.

12th Spiritual Food

I have food to eat that you know nothing about.
John 4.32

I am feeding every day from the spiritual sustenance that has been given to me. I am surrounded by spiritual books, literature and many other resources that provide the conduits for my spiritual nourishment.

Of course, it's one thing to have the food, but for it to benefit me, I need to consume it and take it into myself.

This happens as I meditate and spend time allowing these deep truths to sink into my mind and spirit.

Prayer: Lord, feed me with the bread of heaven.

13th Suffering Many Things

The Son of Man must suffer many things.
Mark 8.31

There is no avoiding suffering in this life. No matter how I try to hedge my life to protect myself from pain it will find a way through.

The life of God incarnate on this earth was marked by suffering and it was through great pain that he achieved his purpose.

Physical and spiritual suffering, discomfort, difficulties and problems are part of life and I can't avoid them. Indeed, I wouldn't want to because they are preparing me for what is yet to come.

Prayer: Lord, thank you that my suffering and pain are all for my ultimate good.

14th End of Ego

I have been crucified.
Galatians 2.20

The Cross of Christ shows me what it means to put to death my ego. What I want is no longer my primary consideration in life.

Paradoxically, the way into real spiritual life is through death, that is death to self. As I walk step by step in the will of God my self-life is constantly realising its death as I go God's way not my way.

My personal ego is no longer running my life as it is nailed down and crucified.

Prayer: Lord, help me to walk in the way of the Cross.

15th Christ Lives

Christ lives in me.
Galatians 2.20

The consciousness of Christ living in me is the most important fact in my life today. It means everything to me because he is the source of every good thing in my life.

It is his inhabitation within my heart that is the spiritual powerhouse in my life. Christ lives and has his life in me as he manifests himself through my life in this world.

Prayer: Jesus, live in me and through me.

16th Next Life

If only for this life.
1 Corinthians 15.19

My whole approach to life has been increasingly built on the conviction that I am not living for this life only.

I am being prepared for my next life through the experience of living my life here and now in this world.

What I do and achieve in this world is of little value apart from its relationship to my eternal destiny.

I am in training for my role in the world to come.

My citizenship is in heaven and my life here on earth is but a preparation for a new life in the new heaven and the new earth.

Prayer: Lord, help me to keep my next world perspective.

17th His Son in Me

God was pleased to reveal His Son in Me.
Galatians 1.16

The personal revelation of God's Son in me was a game-changer in my experience of God. Before that revelation, I had an external faith and I believed in God but when God revealed his Son in me, I knew beyond any shadow of a doubt that he had come to live inside my heart.

My faith moved from being external to being internal.

In this way, my faith was made sure as I knew in the depth of my being that God's Son was now living in me.

Prayer: Lord, continue to increase your self-revelation in me.

18th Upgraded in God

Be transformed by the renewing of your mind.
Romans 12.2

The presence of God's Spirit is having a transforming effect in me. He has entered into my life by coming into my heart and he is working on the inside of me.

Slowly and steadily a transformation is taking place as my old operating system is being replaced by a new one.

I am in a state of constant upgrade and the evidence of this is in the new ways that I see things and the new ways that I respond to life

Prayer: Lord, continue my upgrade in your Spirit today.

19th On Becoming

Plans to prosper you.
Jeremiah 29.11

God's plan for my life is not so much about what I do but about who I am becoming. My plans tend to focus on what I am going to do now or even next year, but his plans are centred around who I am becoming in him.

God's plan is being worked out in me as he develops his life and his character within me. This is his plan and it involves the continuous transformation of my inner self and the conformity of my life into the image of his son.

Prayer: Lord, may I become the person you created me to be.

20th Who I Am

Who do people say that I am?
Mark 8.27

There is a big emphasis in life on what you do. One of the first questions people ask is what do you do?

But God sees things differently from the way things appear outwardly. He looks into my heart and he sees who I really am because he knows the thoughts of my heart.

God is interested in what is going on in my heart. He is concerned with my being not just my doing.

In God's economy who I am is far more important than what I do.

Prayer: Lord, purify my heart.

21st Living on a Prayer

Pray in the Spirit at all times.
Ephesians 6.18

I am carrying a small prayer card in my pocket. It's the prayer of Saint Francis and it's in a little plastic wallet with the prayer on one side and a picture of Francis on the other.

I don't try to read the whole thing I just look to see what I need from it at any particular point in the day.

It may be that I need to be an instrument of peace or maybe there is a need for me to sow pardon, faith or hope. It may be that I need to pray for light in the darkness or the gift of comfort, understanding, love and forgiveness.

The effect of living on this prayer is that it helps me to let go of my self-centred concerns. It takes the focus off me as I set my heart on being an instrument of God's grace, wherever I am.

Prayer: Lord, make me an instrument in your hands.

22nd Letters from Above

You are a letter from Christ.
2 Corinthians 3.3

I am the closest some people are going to get to Christ. I may be one of the only contacts that they have with another person in whom Christ is living and active.

When another person reads me, they are reading my heart where the Spirit of God resides.

I am a living letter of recommendation not written with ink but with the Spirit of the living God in my heart.

Prayer: Lord, may I be a living epistle from Jesus.

23rd Spirit Life

The Spirit gives life.
2 Corinthians 3.6

My spiritual life is not a matter of knowledge, skill or technique. Any competence that I have comes not from myself but from God.

It is the Spirit of God who breathes life into my spirit as I open my heart to him. He is the source of the spiritual life that I experience and share.

Prayer: Lord, increase your Spirit's life within me.

24th Ministry of The Spirit

The ministry of the Spirit.
2 Corinthians 3.8

The opposite of the ministry of the Spirit is the ministry of the flesh. By that, I mean works of service that spring from my own good ideas and best thinking.

The ministry of the Spirit is rooted in my new life, not in my old one. It is built on the new resurrection ground, not on the old creation.

It springs from my new God-given spiritual faculties, power and capacity. It is supernatural rather than natural and it opens up a completely new and different form of ministry.

It is no longer my ministry it is his. It is the ministry of the Spirit.

Prayer: Lord, show me your Spirit's ministry.

25th Wisdom Among the Mature

A message of wisdom among the mature.
1 Corinthians 2.6

God's desire for me as his son is that I grow up and become mature in my faith. As with my natural life so in my spiritual life there is a need for full development and maturity.

This is demonstrated in me as day by day I gain fresh insight into the nature of God, myself, and the world around me.

This is not the wisdom of the world but spiritual wisdom that comes from above as I gain maturity and stature in Christ.

Prayer: Lord, bring me to maturity in my faith.

26th A Need-To-Know Basis

It is not for you to know.
Acts 1.7

When it comes to the guidance of God, I often find that I don't have the full picture. All I have is what I am given by God, and what I have realised is that he operates on a need-to-know basis.

He lets me into enough of the story to enable me to do what I need to do and it is often only after the event that I may gain some understanding of what he has been doing.

Prayer: Lord, help me to follow you even when I don't understand what is happening.

27th Higher Ways

My ways are higher than your ways.
Isaiah 55.9

The way that I would do things is not the way that God does them. God's thoughts and his ways operate on a totally different level from mine.

His perspective is universal and eternal whereas mine is limited and temporal. Before a thought is even on my mind, he knows it completely.

All my mistakes and errors are taken care of through his all-encompassing purposes as he directs my steps and even carries me when I am too overwhelmed to walk alone.

Prayer: Lord, guide me in your higher ways.

28th Living for the Praise

That we might be for the praise of his glory.
Ephesians 1.12

One of the great joys of living a spiritual life is the spirit-given release, ability, and desire to praise God in my heart.

I still find it to be the most extraordinary, surprising and wonderful thing as my praise and love for the Father, the Son and the Holy Spirit well up from inside my heart.

At such times I realise that my main purpose here on earth is to live for the praise of his glory.

Prayer: Lord, I live for the praise of your glory, not mine.

29th Spiritual Intelligence

Spiritually discerned.
1 Corinthians 2.14

At the heart of my spirituality is the notion of spiritual intelligence. This is my God-given capacity to come into and then live in fellowship with God.

Spiritual intelligence, that is the spiritual sensitivity that comes from within, is the fruit of a life that is governed, taught, illumined, and led by the Holy Spirit.

Spiritual intelligence and my spiritual senses are the faculties that enable me to become a spiritual person with capacities, powers and abilities that go far beyond natural apprehension, knowledge or understanding.

Prayer: Holy Spirit, develop your spiritual intelligence within me.

March

1st A Beautiful Thing

The Fellowship of the Holy Spirit.
2 Corinthians 13.14

The fellowship of the Holy Spirit is a beautiful thing. The knowledge and the sense that God is with me, in me and around me is a wonderful gift.

God is not a theory he is an ever-present reality in my life. There is an open heaven so I no longer feel cut off from him.

I am experiencing fellowship with the Holy Spirit as I enjoy his presence. This is a beautiful thing.

Prayer: Lord, thank you for your beautiful presence in my life.

2nd Knowing Him

His son in me.
Galatians 1.16

The knowledge of the presence of Christ and the Holy Spirit in me is the most wonderful thing in the world.

It is more precious to me than anything else. His presence is the most important reality in my life. Nothing else compares with the presence of Jesus because it is priceless and it cannot be bought.

Just knowing that he is alive in me and that I am alive in him is the greatest thing. I am constantly living in this reality of his presence in my heart.

I would not surrender it or exchange it for anything.

Prayer: Thank you Jesus for your presence in my heart.

3rd Ever-Increasing

Ever-increasing glory.
2 Corinthians 3.18

It is a wonderful thing to experience the continual unveiling of Christ in my heart. Day by day and even moment by moment I am able to realise more of his presence within me.

There is a developing revelation of Christ in me as the Holy Spirit is increasingly removing the veil so that I can see Jesus more clearly.

It is a never-ending journey of discovery as the veil is being removed and Jesus is being revealed in me. It is an amazing journey into life.

Prayer: Lord Jesus, continue to unveil your life in my heart.

4th The Mystery

The mystery which is Christ in you.
Colossians 1.27

Every day I am exploring this mystery. It is never-ending and just gets deeper and deeper. This inner territory of my heart is the place of residence for Jesus.

He dwells in my heart and this is a profound mystery.

The realisation of Christ in me and the actualisation of this reality in my every moment living is at the centre of my existence.

Prayer: Holy Spirit, take me deeper into the mystery of Christ in me.

5th Glorious Liberty

The glorious liberty of the children of God.
Romans 8.21

I am experiencing a wonderful sense of spiritual freedom that feels so spacious and limitless.

It is coming to me as my attention is more and more fixed on the revelation of Jesus Christ in my heart.

As I focus on this mystery of Christ in me a new vista is opening up for me. My previous sense of containment and confinement is being replaced by a limitless horizon of hope.

Prayer: Lord, lead me further into your glorious liberty.

6th I Bow Down

Come, let us bow down in worship.
Psalm 95.6

In my heart, I am frequently bowing down and prostrating myself before the Lord Jesus Christ. In my minds-eye, I am bowing my whole self in worship before his presence.

Such is the intensity of my heart's worship for Jesus that there have been times when I have just wanted to fall face down on the pavement and prostrate myself in my worship of him.

I am humbling myself in the presence of the King of the Universe and it feels so right and so good.

Prayer: Lord, thank you that I can worship you with all my heart.

7ᵗʰ A Sense of Wonder

Everyone was gripped with great wonder and awe.
Luke 5.26

I have such a sense of wonder and awe that God came into this world to rescue me from my spiritual infirmity and powerlessness.

I am constantly amazed at his ever-present reality in my life. He doesn't live in temples built by human hands but in the hearts and lives of his people, and that includes me.

He is living in my heart and my body is a temple of his Holy Spirit from which he radiates his life, his power, and his love.

I have not lost my sense of wonder at Jesus. He is truly wonderful and I want to shout it from the housetops.

Prayer: Thank you Jesus for your wonderful rescuing presence in my life.

8ᵗʰ Spiritual Increase

He must increase: I must decrease.
John 3.30

This inward knowledge of Jesus in my heart is an ever-increasing reality in my life. As I surrender to his will, he expands his territory in my heart.

The ground that was previously held by self-will is being given over to him.

It is when life happens and I am taken outside of my ability to cope that Christ is often most manifest within.

Step by step as I walk through life, he takes more ground within my heart. As I let go of my will, my self-life is decreased and it is then that he has the freedom to increase in my heart.

Prayer: Lord, as I decrease may you increase your presence in my heart.

9th Hungry Heart

I have food to eat that you know nothing about.
John 4.32

My new heart is hungry for God. I have an inner drive that is constantly turning me towards him. Like physical hunger, I can't ignore it.

My heart is reaching out for more of him. He is my daily bread and my sustenance. I know what Jesus meant when he said 'I have food to eat that you know nothing about.' It is manna in the wilderness.

This is the spiritual food that my heart cries out for. It is this sustenance, the bread of the presence that feeds my hungry heart.

Prayer: Lord I am hungry for you.

10th Day and Night

Day and night they never stop saying: Holy, holy, holy.
Revelation 4.8

Heart worship is the basis of my life as spontaneous praise rises up within my heart. Some days it becomes a continuous stream of adoration as I worship Jesus, the Holy Spirit and Father God.

At all hours of the day and night, I find that there is a stream of worship flowing from within me.

It is worship and communion with God in my spirit as my heart sings in harmony with the continuous worship in heaven.

There are no limits to worship in heaven. 'Day and night they never stop saying: Holy, holy, holy is the Lord God Almighty. Who was, and is, and is to come.'

Prayer: Lord, enable me to be a continuous worshipper in my heart.

11th God's Own Heart

A man after God's own heart.
1 Samuel 13.14

I am constantly seeking after God's own heart. His heart of love, compassion, joy and peace. These are the qualities that I am making room for in my life.

I am asking him to give me his heart. I am seeking to live from his heart that has been transplanted into me.

I am after his heart in place of mine so that my whole life flows from the centre of his heart.

Prayer: Lord, I am after your heart in mine.

12th The River

Then the angel showed me the river.
Revelation 22.1

I have a secret inner life with God. It is unseen and hidden from all except the Lord. It is a place of constant dialogue with God.

It is the location of conscious contact with the Lord. There is constant two-way communication and dialogue with my Lord.

I am in the river of life. It's a never-ending stream of praise, gratitude and joy in the Lord. This is what life is meant to be, living in fellowship with the Lord.

I'm in the flow of the river of life, the river of God.

Prayer: Lord, help me to stay in the flow of your river of life.

13th A New Heart

I will give you a new heart.
Ezekiel 36.26

Alongside the transfer of the ownership of my life from myself to God, I was given a new heart.

There has been an exchange of heart as my old hardened heart has been replaced by the heart of God. I am not the same person that I used to be.

This is not something that I have done myself as it has been the outcome of Christ dwelling within me.

I have the heart of God living in me.

Prayer: Lord, thank you for my new heart.

14th From the Heart

From the heart.
Matthew 15.19

My best moments flow from the movements of God in my new heart.

As I move out to others from my new heart, I experience God's goodness and compassion flowing from within me.

Instead of trying to love my neighbour, I am really loving them from my heart as I have the same compassion, love and joy for them that I have for myself.

I am now free to be deeply and genuinely pleased or excited by other people's victories and successes as I feel like they are my own.

I think this is what Jesus meant when he said 'love your neighbour as yourself.'

Prayer: Lord, thank you for my new heart of love.

15th Pure in Heart

No guile.
John 1.47

Jesus saw into Nathaniel's heart and observed that he was someone in whom there was no guile.

What he saw in this person was the total absence of darkness. None of the jealousy, secret agendas, deception, manipulation, or schemes of the sophisticated. Jesus commended him for the absolute honesty and purity of his heart and his life.

The Holy Spirit constantly sifts my heart by identifying all impurity in motive, thought, word or deed.

Absolute purity is the Lord's aim for me because it is as my heart is purified of guile that my perception of his reality comes clearly into view.

Prayer: Lord, purify my heart.

16th Spiritually Alive

I am he who is alive.
Revelation 1.18

I am spiritually alive because I have received the resurrection life of Jesus Christ. Jesus has put his resurrection life into me and elevated me from spiritual death into spiritual life.

I am living in the consciousness that 'in Christ', I am alive in a way that I wasn't before. I was spiritually dead, but now I am alive and that life is eternal.

Prayer: Lord thank you that I am spiritually alive for eternity.

17th The Kiss of Life

I was dead.
Revelation 1.18

Before I received the kiss of God's life, I was spiritually dead. Physically I had life, but spiritually, I was without the breath of God within me.

I needed to be raised from spiritual death into spiritual life and this happened when the Spirit of the Lord came into my heart and began to live his life within me.

As he did so, I came to life spiritually as I moved from death to life.

Prayer: Lord, thank you for the gift of spiritual life.

18th Dying to Live

If we died with him, we will be raised with him.
2 Timothy 2.11

To live a resurrection life, I have had to die. Not at a physical level but at the level of my soul and self-life.

My life and my will are constantly being handed over to death, as I die to myself.

It is as my self-life dies that Christ is raised up within me.

Prayer: Lord, help me to live a resurrection life.

19th The Firstborn

The Firstborn.
Colossians 1.18

Through my new birth, I am one of God's new humanity who Jesus referred to as sons.

He is the firstborn among many sons, meaning that he was the first human being to be born into God's new human family.

Jesus is the first human being who God permanently raised from the dead, so he became the firstborn in God's new creation.

Through my new birth, I too have become a son in God's new humanity. I am a member of his new family and the new society that springs from it.

Prayer: Lord, thank you for my sonship in your new family.

20th Our Measure

The Measure of Christ.
Ephesians 4.13

Even in religious systems, success is measured by outward manifestations of size, popularity, influence and apparent impact.

God, on the other hand, is not impressed with such marks of success as seen in the outward appearance of things.

The thing that matters to him is Christ and the measure of Christ that is in me and in you. Success from God's perspective is measured by the extent to which Christ is formed in us.

When it comes to success what counts with God is how much of Christ there is in you and me.

Prayer: Lord Jesus, more of you in me.

21st A Different Pressure

Conformed to the Image of his Son.
Romans 8.29

There is a lot of pressure to conform to our culture and there are many social conventions that we are expected to follow.

The Holy Spirit exercises a different pressure to conform, not to contemporary culture, but to the image of his Son, Jesus.

God exerts his pressure on the inside, in my spirit. It is from this vantage point that he operates from within me to conform me to the image of his son.

Prayer: Lord, conform me to the image of your son.

22nd The Weakness of God

The Weakness of God.
1 Corinthians 1.25

I am not pumped up with my own physical, intellectual or emotional strength and I am keenly aware of my weakness.

Even the great Apostle said that he came to people in weakness, fear and with much trembling.

This weakness of God that I too experience is the very place where God's strength becomes most manifest in my life.

It is in my weakness, fear, and trembling that I find God's strength and courage to face opposition and threats.

Prayer: Lord, in my weakness, be strong.

23rd Never Perceiving

Ever seeing but never perceiving.
Mark 4.12

The great tragedy of this world is that so many people never become conscious of God and they never perceive him.

They are forever seeing spiritual realities but never perceiving God in them. God for them is an external rather than an internal reality.

I knew about God and Jesus because I had read the Bible, but I knew nothing of the living and loving relationship that was on offer within its pages. I was seeing but not perceiving.

As I started to see he ripped open my heart, reached into my innermost being and touched me with his life.

Prayer: Lord, open the eyes of my heart.

24th Real Wisdom

The world through its wisdom did not know God.
1 Corinthians 1.21

True knowledge of God has not come to me through my intellect. Intellectual knowledge brings insight and information but what it does not deliver is an experimental knowledge of God.

God can only be truly known by revelation as he reveals himself to me in my heart. The tiniest fragment of truth as it is revealed in my heart has the power to bring me deeper into my knowledge of him.

It's not the amount of information that counts, it's what I do with it that matters. As I receive his wisdom at depth, I come to know more of God's reality in my heart. This is the wisdom of God.

Prayer: Lord, give me true wisdom in a deep knowledge of you.

25th Not Found Here

The Kingdom of God.
1 Corinthians 4.20

There are lots of things that just don't exist in the Kingdom of God and they cannot be found there.

In the Kingdom of God, there is no more death or disease or illness. There is no more anxiety, fear, worry or insecurity. There is no more stress, pressure, pain or sadness.

Instead, there is life, true peace, genuine love, kindness, goodness and gentleness.

Prayer: Lord, may your Kingdom come in my life.

26th Waiting with God

Wait for the Lord.
Psalm 27.14

Waiting is an action but it is one of the most difficult ones to do because when the pressure is on, everything within my soul wants to act and do something.

Ungoverned and unrestrained my soul force presses me on as it wants me to act and to act now. It just can't wait and it is prone to be panicky or fear-driven.

Waiting is a powerful spiritual activity because of its intentionality. When I am waiting for the Lord, I am waiting for the right time and the right way forward.

When the time is right, I will know it.

Prayer: Lord, help me to wait on you.

27th Fossilised Remains

As in Adam all die, so in Christ will all be made alive.
1 Corinthians 15.22

God will not bring life to my old nature. The natural or old man after Adam is dead and buried in Christ.

All I have now are the fossilised remains of my old nature in the form of habits that are the emotional, physical and mental relics of my old life.

God has given me an entirely new life and a new start. It is this new man that is being blessed and developed. Jesus only brings life where the new man lives and that's in me through his Spirit within.

Prayer: Lord, pour your resurrection life into me.

28th Resurrection Power

Sons of disobedience.
Ephesians 2.2

It is only through God's resurrection power within me that I can say 'thy will not my will be done.'

My, won't power can be stronger than my will power as my ego continues to argue with God and his will for my life.

Like a child having a tantrum and stamping its feet my innate resistance to God is a powerful force.

It is only through a power greater than myself, which is the life of God within me, that I can say, 'thy will, not mine, be done.'

Prayer: Lord, overcome my resistance to you.

29th Manifesting His Presence

It is no longer I who live, but Christ who lives in me.
Galatians 2.20

I am here to manifest the presence of Christ in this world. The only way that this is going to happen is if I get myself out of the way.

It is his life within me that is seeking expression in my everyday life in this world.

I start each day by clearing up the rubbish and removing the trash from the previous day. I seek to remove the obstacles in me that are hindering the manifestation of the presence of the living Christ from within

In this way, it is no longer I who live, but Christ who lives in me.

Prayer: Lord Jesus, live in and through my life.

30th Reckon Yourself Dead

Reckon yourself dead to sin but alive to God.
Romans 6.11

Death to self does not sound that great but it is the doorway into real freedom and life with God.

I have been crucified with Christ and the life that I now live is that which is supplied to me as Christ lives in and through me.

It's not my life that I am living but his life as I surrender more of myself and become increasingly available to him.

Prayer: Lord, help me to die to self and to live for you.

31st Self-Denial

Whoever would come after me must deny himself.
Mark 8.34

The idea of self-denial is a difficult one to sell in our culture. The spirit of the age urges us towards self-fulfilment rather than the denial of the self.

As I go on in this journey with Christ the road is getting narrower and steeper. The only way that I can continue up this narrow lane is by jettisoning any excess baggage that I am still carrying.

I am having to let go of my cherished habits and ways of being as I surrender to the will of my Lord. These things have to go for me to move forward.

My innate self-centeredness is being eroded by the internal pressure of Christ within me. Increasingly it is no longer I who live but Christ who lives within me.

Prayer: Lord, release me from the bondage of self.

April

1st Your Ways

Your ways, my ways.
Isaiah 55.8

Rather than going my own way without God, I am now living in cooperation with the Lord. I am going with God rather than against him. I am going his way rather than my way.

This does have its difficulties and there are struggles, but these are nothing in comparison to the problems that come with refusing to cooperate with God.

As I go his way, I find that my life works in a way that it never did before.

Prayer: Lord, help me to go with you rather than against you.

2nd The Fashion of this World

Do not be conformed to the fashions of this world.
Romans 12.2

Instead of following the way of Christ, it is so much easier to fit in with the fashions of this world.

We absorb the looks, ideas and values of the world around us so that we become almost indistinguishable from the culture that we inhabit.

Without realising it, I can almost unconsciously follow the fashions and ways of this world instead of standing apart and being the person, he is calling me to be.

In Christ, I am distinctive and different because I am one of his resurrection people. I am a new man who is increasingly conforming to the fashions and ways of a new world order in him.

Prayer: Lord, help me to conform to your new world order.

3rd Fear of Tomorrow

Do not worry beforehand.
Matthew 10.19

I have to think about tomorrow and plan for the future but I don't have to worry about it unless I want to.

In thinking about the future and situations where I wonder if I will be able to cope, Jesus instructs me not to worry beforehand about what I will say or do.

In my anticipation, I need not fear any real or imagined future event.

I can trust that God is sufficient and that he will give me whatever I need to meet any situation that life can throw at me.

Prayer: Lord, teach me not to worry about the future.

4th Seize the Day

This is the day the Lord has made: let us rejoice and be glad in it.
Psalm 118.24

I am seeking to live in the day and to enjoy each day of my life as a gift from God. Rather than seeing the day as something to be got through or endured I endeavour to see it as an opportunity to express my joy in the Lord.

As I rejoice in the Lord in my heart, I find that gratitude rises up and I can enjoy the day as a gift rather than a burden.

Prayer: Lord, help me to rejoice in each day of life.

5th A New Creation

If anyone is in Christ, he is a new creation, the old has gone and the new has come.
2 Corinthians 5.17

I am a new creation in Christ. The old has gone and the new has come. The old man of the flesh was crucified with Christ and the new man of the Spirit has been raised to life by him.

My old self was demolished, it was finished, it died and was buried with Christ. Having died with Christ, I have now been raised up with him from the dead.

I am a new man, a new creation in Christ and I am living a completely new life. The old has gone and the new has come.

Prayer: Lord, thank you for my new life and my new creation in Christ.

6th Back to Life

You were dead.
Ephesians 2.1

In my natural state, I was a fallen spirit that had lost its connection and communion with God. In my unregenerate state, my fallen human spirit still existed but it was separated from God and I was spiritually dead.

When I believed in Jesus I was born again and my spirit was brought to life as it was raised from the dead by the Spirit of God.

Regeneration began in my spirit as I received the uncreated life of the Lord that I was originally designed to receive.

My spirit is now raised from its fallen state and I am alive to God, connected and in communion with him.

Prayer: Lord, thank you for bringing my spirit back to life.

7th New Wineskin

You cannot put new wine in old wineskins.
Mark 2.22

To be able to receive the new wine of God's life, I needed to have my spirit renewed. I needed a new container as the old one was not able to hold the presence or power of the Spirit of God.

God's answer is the new wineskin that is my renewed spirit which can take the pressure and fermentation from the new wine of his indwelling Spirit.

My human spirit was dead, hardened, and inflexible, not able to receive the power of God. But God regenerated my spirit so that it can receive his life, energy and power without exploding.

Prayer: Lord, thank you for the new wineskin and your new wine.

8th The Prime Mover

He convinces the world.
John 16.8

My spirit is being regenerated by God's life that is flowing into me. The Holy Spirit is the prime mover in my regeneration as he applies the work of the cross to my experience of life.

The Holy Spirit abides in me and does his work of renewal by bringing life to my previously dead spirit.

The entire personality of the Holy Spirit is abiding in me. He is not just visiting he is dwelling in me on a permanent basis.

He is living in my house, he is a permanent resident, he is the source of my spiritual energy and he is in charge.

Prayer: Lord, continue your life-giving work in me.

9th Spiritual Ability

> *A new spirit.*
> *Ezekiel 36.26*

I have an intuitive knowledge of the Lord that is being given to me and expanded as I surrender to the movement of his Spirit within me.

I have a new spirit in me and it is one that I wasn't born with.

Within me, there is my human spirit that has been awoken from its coma and brought back to life.

The Spirit of God has come into me as a permanent resident to work resurrection life in me from the inside out.

Prayer: Lord, increase your resurrection life within me.

10th More will be Given

> *To the one who has more will be given.*
> *Matthew 13.12*

This has always seemed unfair to me from my human perspective but it is an important principle in the Kingdom of God.

The reason I receive more of God's life, presence and revelation is because I have already opened myself to receiving the life of his Spirit within me.

I go to meetings and I find that God is giving me revelation whereas the person next to me might be quite unaware of God doing anything at all.

God is giving me more as he is revealing things and showing me things that I didn't see before. I am continually being given more revelation and knowledge of him because I have gratefully embraced, as well as acted on what I have received from him so far.

Prayer: Lord, thank you that you are always ready to give me more of yourself.

11th Living out of the New

The new has come.
2 Corinthians 5.17

I am no longer focussing on the old man of my flesh. Instead, my attention is increasingly focused on the new regenerate man of my spirit through whom God is revealing his Holy presence. I am learning to honour God's Holy presence.

I am now willing to allow him to work through me and not block him by the imposition of my will.

The Holy Spirit is in my spirit and I am saying yes to him as he works from within me.

Prayer: Lord, help me to live out of your new life in me.

12th New Life

All things have become new.
2 Corinthians 5.17

My new birth was the beginning of a new life for me. It was just the start of a life that is constantly expanding and developing.

My spiritual life is a never-ending journey of discovery and learning.

I am a disciple, that is one who is under discipline. I am, as a friend of mine says, in 'training for reigning.'

Everything flows from the new birth and it can't be bypassed.

Prayer: Lord, thank you for the gift of new birth.

13th No Bypass

You must be born again.
John 3.7

The vessel for the reception of God's Spirit into me is my spirit which had to undergo what Jesus describes as a new birth.

There was no bypassing this and I could not make any spiritual progress until I received this new birth.

When I was born again my spirit came alive and I began to be able to receive the life of God's Spirit into my spirit in a way that had not been possible before.

Prayer: Lord, thank you for my new birth.

14th No Longer Two Lives

It is no longer I who live.
Galatians 2.20

There are no longer two lives to be lived but one. I have been bought at a price and the life that I live is no longer mine.

I am not trying to live my own life whilst living for God at the same time. That approach does not work because there will always be tension and conflict between my life and his purposes.

Trying to live two lives is hard and it doesn't work so now I am not seeking to live two lives but just one.

This one is rooted firmly in the will and purposes of God.

Prayer: Lord, help me to live the life that you have laid out for me.

15th Bondservant

A bondservant of Jesus Christ.
Romans 1.1

I am a bondservant of Jesus Christ. My life is no longer my own as I have willingly given my life in service to the master.

A bondservant is one who has been given their freedom but has chosen to stay on in the Master's house in the role of a servant.

I have been given my freedom as I have been set free from the law of sin and death and as a result of this, I have been able to enter into service in God's household as a bondservant.

Prayer: Lord, make me a good servant of Jesus Christ.

16th Discipline

The Lord disciplines those he loves.
Hebrews 12.6

These two things go together as I seek to live by the Spirit. I am under discipline and instruction as I walk by the Spirit each day.

Sometimes lessons come at me thick and fast whereas at other times there are periods of more gentle instruction.

This is a very considered way of life as I seek to follow my master.

Prayer: Lord, thank you for your daily discipline and instruction.

17th The Divine Builder

Unless the Lord builds the house.
Psalm 127.1

God only dwells in houses that he has built. He has strict and particular requirements for his habitation and he won't put up with shoddy buildings.

As with the temple of old the Lord dwells in the holy of holies which is now located within our spirit.

The Holy Spirit cannot make his home in my flesh, he can only live in my spirit at the centre of the house behind the walls of my thoughts, feelings and will.

Prayer: Lord, build this house.

18th Building from Within

Do you not know that God's Spirit dwells in you?
1 Corinthians 3.16

The Holy Spirit is a person who is inhabiting the Holy of Holies of my spirit and it is from this position that he is constantly seeking to bring me into a deeper experience of the reality of Christ.

Through my faith in Jesus Christ, I am regenerated but it is my obedience to the Holy Spirit from his place of habitation in my spirit that determines my spiritual development.

Whilst the cross destroys all that comes from Adam the Holy Spirit builds in what comes from Christ.

Being spiritual involves knowing the Holy Spirit at work experimentally as he delivers me from the oppression of my soul and body.

Prayer: Holy Spirit, continue your building work in my spirit.

19th Oppression

Those who are oppressed
Luke 4.18

The biggest spiritual conflict that I have is not external but internal as my flesh wages war against the Holy Spirit in my spirit.

My soul wars with my spirit by using my flesh to contain and restrain my inner man of the spirit.

Ungoverned my soul binds and contains my spirit man so that my flesh can maintain control of my life.

Within me the Holy Spirit finds himself being oppressed and suppressed by my flesh as I seek to impose my will, my ways and my thinking onto him.

Prayer: Lord, free me from the oppression of my soul.

20th One in Spirit

One Spirit
1 Corinthians 6.17

My union with Jesus Christ is between his Spirit and my spirit. This union and connection between myself and the Lord take place in the inner man of my spirit.

The fruit of this union is made manifest through my body and soul as I live out of the place of union in my spirit.

It is from this wellspring that my spiritual life is constantly being refreshed and developed.

Prayer: Lord, thank you for my spiritual union with Jesus Christ.

21st Going Against Myself

Let us throw off everything that hinders
Hebrews 12.1

In some areas of my life, I am being asked by God to go against myself and my own will.

The Holy Spirit has been leaning on me and suggesting to me that I need to let go of some things that I have been holding onto and that have been holding me back.

For reasons that I don't fully understand God wants these things out of my life.

My will, my mind and my body are attached to these behaviours and yet the Spirit within me is saying that I need to let them go.

I am saying 'okay God, I don't understand why but I am going to resist my flesh and hand this area of my life over to you.'

Prayer: Lord, I let go of my way and my will.

22nd Surrender All

Leaving all things.
Luke 5.28

The hymn 'All to Jesus I surrender' has been running through my mind and as it does so, I sense that the Holy Spirit is encouraging me to let go of anything I am holding onto instead of Him.

It is the call for me to surrender all to Jesus.

The hymn's chorus, 'I surrender all', is speaking to me about the continual handing over of my will and my life to him so that I can increasingly know the sacred flame that is burning within my spirit.

Prayer: Jesus, I surrender all of myself to you.

23rd Spirit Centred

Live by the Spirit.
Galatians 5.16

I am discovering that the key to life is found in living a spirit-centred rather than a self-centred life.

In all the decisions of life, I have two choices. God's way or my way? Self-centred or Spirit-centred?

When I am Spirit-centred I am submitting my whole self to God. I am placing myself under the authority, tuition and discipline of the Holy Spirit rather than operating purely on the basis of my own thoughts, desires and feelings.

Prayer: Lord, help me to live a Spirit-centred life.

24th Freedom

> *It is for freedom that Christ has set us free.*
> *Galatians 5.1*

There is a wonderful sense of freedom that comes to me as I walk in the Spirit. It is almost as if I am soaring like an eagle, ascending on the thermals of God's breath.

Although from the outside it looks ordinary this is an extraordinary life as I live from the movement of God's Spirit within.

The more my self-life is displaced by the Spirit's life the greater the lift, as the Spirit of God sets me free from my bondage to this world and all its troubles.

Prayer: Lord, thank you for my freedom in Christ.

25th Spiritual Advance

> *To will and to do.*
> *Philippians 2.13*

In regeneration God gave me a new spiritual life and then his Spirit was able to indwell my renewed spirit.

His Spirit reveals Christ in me as he sanctifies me and leads me onwards into new and higher ground.

It is as I honour the Holy Spirit's presence and allow Him to work in me that I find myself advancing in my spiritual life.

Prayer: Holy Spirit, I am willing for you to work within me.

26th The Crucified Life

Cut it off.
Matthew 5.30

The cross is cutting into my flesh. My flesh is under assault from the Spirit of the Lord within me.

My flesh is crucified as I surrender my will and my way to God's will and God's way. The cross is being applied to my flesh life, and as I surrender to it, it is cutting away everything that is standing in the way of my spiritual usefulness.

I am experiencing soul surgery and the cross is God's surgical knife which he wields with great precision.

Prayer: Lord, thank you for the cross.

27th His Drum Beat

If the Lord wills, we will live and do this.
James 4.15

As a bondservant of Jesus Christ, I am no longer free to do as I want. My life is not my own as I am a servant awaiting my master's orders.

I am attending to him and as a result, my life is no longer my own in the way that it used to be. I am no longer self-determining because what I do and where I go are governed by the master.

He is the boss not me and I now march to the beat of his drum rather than my own.

Prayer: Lord, keep me marching to the beat of your drum, not mine.

28th Small Things

The day of small things.
Zechariah 4.10

I tend to think that God is only concerned with the broader ways and bigger issues in my life. Some things seem just too small or too trivial for God to be getting involved in, but this is not the case.

In numerous small ways, the Lord reminds me that he is closely involved in the details of my life.

God continues to remind me of his presence when he meets some intimate need that only he could know about.

Prayer: Lord, reveal yourself to me in small things.

29th Trusting the Lord

Trust in the Lord with all your heart, and do not lean on your own understanding.
Proverbs 3.5

My default setting is to trust in myself rather than trust in God's wisdom and provision. I tend to look for human solutions and strategies before consulting the Lord.

How much time and energy do I waste in trying to solve problems myself before I admit that I just can't do it by unaided willpower or human skill and ability?

Life is so much better and easier when I truly hand all things over to the Lord. It's hard to let go of my self-sufficiency and allow God to take care of things, but that is what he loves to do if I will just get out of the way and let him be God.

Prayer: Lord, I trust in you rather than in myself.

30th The Lord's Discipline

Do not make light of the Lord's discipline.
Hebrews 12.5

My life is under the scrutiny of the Lord as he disciplines me and trains me in his ways. I am a disciple under discipline in the school of the Spirit as I am being trained for eternity.

The Holy Spirit is my personal trainer who is with me at all times of the day and night. This is boot camp, it's a full-on training program and there is no time off.

The Lord uses every situation in life as a learning opportunity as he leads me deeper in obedience and selfless service.

Nothing is wasted in God's economy as I submit to his discipline.

Prayer: Lord, disciple me in the ways of your Kingdom.

May

1st God's Thoughts

But we have the mind of Christ.
1 Corinthians 2.16

I am slowly learning the art of tuning in to God's thoughts. I am seeking to develop an ever-increasing awareness of the mind of the Lord in any and every situation of life.

What is he thinking about this person? Where is he working in these particular circumstances? What is his thought and is he asking me to participate in any way?

The Lord may give me a word of encouragement for someone or I might be directed to pray.

This is the development of God-consciousness.

Prayer: Jesus, may I have your mind in all of life's circumstances.

2nd Focus

This world is passing away.
1 John 2.17

In the past, I have focused and fixed my attention on people, places or things. My time and resources have been heavily invested in them.

I am still interested in people but my desire to spend time on hobbies or pastimes has greatly diminished.

I have less and less interest in this world as my gaze is increasingly fixed on the life of the world to come.

These days my focus is on the new heaven and the new earth.

Prayer: Lord, keep my gaze firmly fixed on you.

3rd Change

Change, for the Kingdom of God is at hand.
Matthew 3.2

To repent means to change and therefore my life as a disciple is one of continual change. I am not the same person that I used to be.

I have changed and I am changing. I am in the process of transformation as the Spirit of the Lord moves in my spirit.

Some people are never going to change. They can't because deep down they don't want to. Their will is nailed to a particular way and so no progress is possible.

Prayer: Lord, I embrace the change that you bring into my life.

4th Things Above

Set your affections on things above.
Colossians 3.2

It seems that slowly and steadily I am being stripped of all earthly attachments. Piece by piece my self-centred desires are being eroded and then removed as God increasingly takes centre stage in my life.

This is not something that I am doing myself. It is entirely God's work as he is preparing me for my future life with him.

Nothing of my old self is fit for the kingdom of heaven and that is why it is being removed.

Prayer: Lord, set my affections on things above.

5th Beyond Ability

Beyond our ability.
2 Corinthians 1.8

There are some things on the horizon of my life that I feel are way beyond my ability to cope with.

I don't feel up to dealing with them and I am at a loss to know how I can prepare myself for the things that are coming my way.

I am being brought face to face with the limits of my self-reliance. I know that in and of myself I do not have the necessary resources. Thankfully God does and I am trusting that through the testing times ahead he will teach me how to rely on him in ways that I have never known before.

Prayer: Lord, teach me to rely on you as never before.

6th Strengthen what Remains

Strengthen the things that remain.
Revelation 3.2

All that will last into eternity is what is of Christ. Only what is in and of Christ has any eternal value. Everything will be tested by fire and everything that is not of him will be burned up.

This is why everything in me that is not of him needs to be denied and everything in me that is of him needs to be strengthened.

As I cooperate with Christ within me everything that is of him is being built up and developed so that it will remain.

Prayer: Lord, strengthen the things that remain.

7th Your Affections

Set your affections on things above.
Colossians 3.2

This is a big battle for me as I am so locked into the things and desires of this ever-present material world.

My focus is so rooted in this life and this world with its lusts and pleasures that it can seem impossible to disengage.

It is only as the Spirit of the Lord moves within me that I am being weaned off this world and its powerful but passing desires.

Prayer: Lord, reset my affections on things above.

8th Pure Gold

Pure Gold.
1 Peter 1.7

The refiner's fire is a work in me. Its flames are continually burning away the impurity and dross from within me. I am being tested, proven, sifted and tried by the fire of God.

The mass of solid impurities that float to the surface of my life in the furnace of God's presence is being removed.

Like gold refined in the fire the Lord repeatedly puts me back in the furnace of affliction and worldly troubles so that the quality of my eternal spirit can be purified and increased.

Prayer: Lord, refine and purify my heart.

9th Progress Not Perfection

Be Perfect.
Matthew 5.48

Jesus never lowered the bar in terms of our behaviour but what he did do was to provide for our weakness and failure.

His standards are absolute and that is why he provided a way out for us because perfection will always elude us.

He not only paid the penalty for our failure but provided the route to a new way of living. The life of Christ in me provides a constant force and power for good that step by step overcomes the old man of the flesh.

Prayer: Lord, progress my life in you.

10th Death

Death is at work in you.
2 Corinthians 4.12

Christ can only live in me because I have died. Not physically but spiritually I died when I was baptised into Christ.

My old self-life died and my new life began as I was spiritually raised with Christ and seated with Him in heavenly places.

This is all true but much of it has yet to be realised in my experience. God's Spirit of wisdom and revelation is at work in me as I learn to die to self and to live for Christ.

Prayer: Lord, may I die to myself and live for you.

11th The Abolition of 'I'.

No longer I, but Christ.
Galatians 2.20

The abolition of 'I' puts a question mark over all my 'I' statements. I want, I think, I need, I will not, and I don't want, are just a sample of the self-life that Christ in me is waging war with.

The abolition of 'I' is a process that never ends as I say yes to the ascendancy of Christ in me.

Prayer: Lord, I say yes to Christ within me.

12th Greater Than

He that is in you is greater.
1 John 4.4

The presence and positive pressure of Christ within my spirit are greater than the outside forces that are seeking to pull me away from him.

My weaknesses are well known to the enemy and he fights dirty. He exploits every weakness and every wound to get me to capitulate to his wishes.

In times of pressure, I need to remind myself and the enemy that Christ in me is greater than he that is in the world.

Prayer: Lord, be strong in me.

13th But Christ

But Christ.
Galatians 2.20

I want to do things that are contrary to the will of Christ within me. There is a desire within my old self to gratify the pressure that I am feeling from my flesh. My mind is under the sway of temptation and I could easily give way.

But Christ is in me and he is giving me the strength to say no to self and yes to him. It's 110lbs pressure on the inside and 100lbs on the outside so that's enough to keep me in his way.

Prayer: Jesus, keep me in the power of choice.

14th In Love

In love with this present world.
2 Timothy 4.10

Like the gravitational pull of the moon on the oceans of this planet, the world exerts a powerful force over all of us.

I am not immune from the attractions and addictions that are constantly calling for my attention and affection.

The habits of my former life die hard and it is all too easy to be seduced back into the old-scented ways.

Like the deceptive but seductive voices of the sirens of old the world and its pleasures are calling to me from the rocks of destruction. I don't want to go there.

Prayer: Lord, may I love you more than this world.

15th The Gardner

My father is the gardener.
John 15.1

God is working in the garden of my heart as he is weeding out everything that is not of Christ. He only plants and grows his life in the soil of my new nature in Christ and therefore the weeds of my old life before Christ have been gradually exposed and removed.

My old patterns of life and thinking are like weeds in my garden that left unattended would eventually take over and ruin all the good work that the Lord has done.

Prayer: Lord, weed the garden of my heart.

16th Every Branch

He removes every branch in me that does not bear fruit.
John 15.2

I have always thought about this as a personal thing as God is pruning and cutting away everything in me that does not bear fruit.

This is true but it has a wider meaning. Christian assemblies of all kinds are expected to bear fruit and can expect to be pruned and severely cut back so that they can bear fruit.

Just as in my own spiritual life there are times of growth and then cutting back so in the church as the Lord removes every branch that does not bear fruit.

Prayer: Lord, make us fruitful.

17th This Foundation

This Foundation.
1 Corinthians 3.12

There is only one foundation for building the work of God in this world and that foundation is Christ.

All work of eternal value is founded and built on him.

The questions that I ask myself about all that I am seeking to do for the Lord are these. Is it of Christ? How much of Christ is in this thing? Is this thing that I am doing rooted and grounded in him or is it something that has come from my independent thinking and imagination?

Only what is of Christ will last as everything else will be tested by fire and burned up.

Prayer: Lord, may my work be all of Christ and not of self.

18th Grounded in Christ

Rooted and Grounded.
Ephesians 3.17

I thank God that I am firmly rooted and grounded in Christ. From this secure position, everything in me that is not of him and that makes me unstable is being slowly and steadily removed.

The only choice I have now is whether to give up my self-life willingly and joyfully or to have it removed the hard way.

The way in is the way on and the way in was Christ so the way on is Christ. As I cooperate with his Holy Spirit, he is building me up from the foundation of Christ within me.

It is from this solid ground of Christ in me that my life is being reconstructed.

Prayer: Lord, keep me firmly rooted and grounded in Christ.

19th The Whole Measure

The whole measure of the fullness of Christ.
Ephesians 4.13

Spiritual maturity involves attaining the whole measure of the fullness of Christ. It means being filled up with Christ to the point of fullness.

That's quite a vision for my life and it is what I aspire to. My goal is not to fill my life with things but to be filled with Christ.

There are to be no half-measures when it comes to having Christ in me. I want to be filled up to overflowing with his life. What more could I ask for?

Prayer: Lord, fill me with the whole measure of Christ.

20th New for Old

Put off your old self, put on the new self.
Ephesians 4.22-4

My former way of life left me with habits and ways of living that are no longer fit for purpose.

As I grow into Christ, I am being instructed to put off my old self because it is constantly being corrupted by its deceitful desires.

I am not only putting off the old self but putting on the new self which has been created to be like God in true holiness and righteousness.

New for old is the exchange that is constantly taking place in my heart and life. What a brilliant exchange this is!

Prayer: Lord, help me to put off the old self and put on the new.

21st Unholy Trinity

Sensuality, impurity and lust.
Ephesians 4.19

This unholy trinity of my old life before Christ has to be rejected if I am to continue to walk and live in the light of Christ.

The main downside of living in the old self of sensuality, impurity and lust is that it never truly satisfies.

Indulgence and sensuality just produce addiction and an ever-increasing desire for more impurity.

The worst consequence of this unholy alliance is the hardness of heart and loss of spiritual sensitivity that it brings.

Prayer: Lord, help me to keep walking in the light.

22nd Flaming Arrows

The flaming arrows of the evil one.
Ephesians 6.16

Sometimes, I find myself under an assault from the evil one. This world is a spiritual battleground and as a disciple of Christ, I am a legitimate target for the enemy.

There are times when for reasons that I don't fully understand I find myself on the receiving end of a sustained missile attack.

Temptations and tests in my life circumstances bring me to near breaking point as the enemy of my soul launches yet another assault on my life.

He wants to bring me down in whatever way he can and he will use any weapon at his disposal to take me out.

As long as I stay sheltered under the Lord's shield of faith, I am safe.

Prayer: Lord, thank you for your shield of faith.

23rd Wait

Wait for the gift.
Acts 1.4

The world is determined to take the waiting out of wanting as we are constantly being offered tomorrow's bread today.

Following his ascension into heaven, Jesus instructed his disciples to wait in the city before doing anything else.

Waiting can be the hardest thing in the world especially if we are champing at the bit to get on with our latest scheme or plan.

The disciples had to wait for the gift, that is the power to do the work that the Lord was calling them to do.

Prayer: Lord, help me to wait for you.

24th Fill All Things

That he might fill all things.
Ephesians 4.10

God's plan is that Christ should fill all things in every way and that includes me. He intends for me to attain the whole measure of the fullness of Christ.

Christ is seated at the right hand of God the Father in the heavenly realms and he has been appointed to be the supreme head over everything, to bring everything under his authority, and to fill everything with his fullness.

My aim is to be filled with Christ so that I manifest his presence and express his reality in this world.

Prayer: Lord, fill me with Christ.

25th Wash Me

Purge me with hyssop, and I shall be clean; wash me.
Psalm 51.7

The reference to hyssop refers to both spiritual and physical cleansing of the human soul and flesh.

Physically, hyssop is a type of herb that has antiseptic and powerful cleansing properties.

Spiritually, it has been used to sprinkle the sacrificial blood in the process of atonement for sin.

In both of these capacities, it serves as a means of purification from the physical and spiritual consequences of sin.

The words 'purge me' are a heart cry from an ancient king who was sick and tired of himself. It's a cry for God's cleansing and renewal.

It's a prayer that I pray too, especially when I am sick and tired of my sinful human soul.

Prayer: Lord, purge me.

26th The Dictatorship of Ego

Slaves to the one whom you obey.
Romans 6.16

The power of self-will is still exerting itself in my life. For so long it was used to calling the shots and dictating what, when, and how things should and ought to be done in my life.

My self-life rooted in my ego has been dethroned but it still has the sense that God is a usurper and therefore my ego makes repeated attempts to overthrow the government of God in my life.

Old habits reinforced by ego are a particular problem as they can all too easily seize control and start to dictate my behaviour in ways that are destructive to my walk with God.

Prayer: Lord, keep me from the dictatorship of my ego.

27th Footholds

Do not give the enemy a foothold.
Ephesians 4.27

Climbers without secure footholds fall off and it is the same with the enemy of our souls. He wants to find footholds so that he can cling to our lives and weigh us down.

Depression and feelings of guilt or shame as well as obtrusive thoughts are all part of the enemy's tactics to knock us out.

I am seeking to deal with those weak places in the rock face of my life where the enemy has managed to get a foothold.

Prayer: Lord, may there be no footholds for the enemy in my life.

28th No Settling in Babylon

My soul longs for the courts of the Lord.
Psalm 84.2

When God's people were taken into exile in Babylon many of them were just assimilated into the culture.

They settled down and became part of the life of the city. They were not looking for anything more or anything different and got on with their ordinary lives.

At the same time, there was a remnant longing for God's presence. Material satisfaction was not enough as in their hearts they longed for God.

These were the people who God used to rebuild the ancient ruins and to restore the honour of his name.

Prayer: Lord, may I rebuild the ancient ruins.

29th Out of Egypt

Out of Egypt have I called my son.
Matthew 2.15

I have been brought out of the spiritual bondage that was represented by Egypt but like God's people of old, Egypt is still not out of me.

Although physically separated from my former ways of life I have found that my heart is still spiritually prone to look back.

Of course, I look back with rose-tinted glasses as I all too easily forget the painful struggles and difficulties that I had in my old life before Christ.

Thankfully, life's challenges including some long seasons of testing in the wilderness have greatly reduced my hankering after Egypt as my focus has increasingly been on the promised land beyond the Jordan.

Prayer: Lord, lead me further into your promised land.

30th Positive Faith

Although the fig tree shall not blossom, I will rejoice.
Habakkuk 3.17

My faith is positive in the sense that whatever happens to me, I am going on with God.

No matter what mistakes I make or failures I encounter I have put my life completely into the hands of God.

I am entirely for God and my life is now at his disposal. I am not living to pursue any worldly interests and I am now only here for the Lord.

Prayer: Lord, I am here for you and you only.

31st Inward Longing

My soul thirsts, for the living God.
Psalm 42.2

I have an underlying and uncomfortable Godly dissatisfaction with the state of things as they are.

I carry a sense of inner longing for something more than the spiritual conditions and the measure of Christ that I experience around me.

I believe that this inner desire for more, and my sense of spiritual need is God-given. This spiritual sense of longing is healthy as it keeps me seeking and searching for his presence and life.

Prayer: Lord, I long for you in a dry and weary land.

June

1st Living in the Centre

Teach me your paths.
Psalm 25.4

It feels so good to be living in the centre of God's will for my life. In the past, I have spent a lot of time wandering close to the edge or even outside of God's will, but these days I seek to stay in the centre.

As I live from the centre of God's will for my life, things run a lot more smoothly. This does not mean that there are no problems or difficulties, indeed there are often more challenging circumstances as I follow the Lord.

But I know that even in difficult times the best place for me to be is right in the centre of God's will.

Prayer: Lord, help me to be centred in your will.

2nd Spiritual Ground

Rooted and grounded.
Ephesians 3.17

It has taken me a lifetime to begin to understand the importance of living my life on spiritual ground rather than on natural ground.

Living on a spiritual basis means that I am seeking to live from within rather than having to rely solely on the natural human wisdom of this world.

Living on spiritual ground means offering up every sphere of life to be directed by the Spirit of the Lord who dwells within me.

Prayer: Lord, help me to live on a spiritual basis.

3rd Spiritual Capacities

We have not received the spirit of the world.
1 Corinthians 2.12

It is the indwelling of the Spirit of God within me that gives me the spiritual capacity for knowing and seeing the things of God.

This faculty for spiritual knowledge and spiritual sensing is part of the ever-expanding inward revelation of Jesus Christ.

Spiritual increase and advance come to me through fresh revelations of Jesus Christ in my heart.

Prayer: Lord, expand my spiritual capacity.

4th Weaned off the World

Love not the world.
1 John 2.15

Slowly and steadily, I am being weaned off this world. The worldly trophies and ambitions that used to grip me have mostly faded away.

Many of the things that used to occupy my attention and energy have lost their taste and no longer hold my interest.

Increasingly my attention is focused on eternity and heavenly pursuits, as the things of this world grow strangely dim in the light of his glory and grace.

Prayer: Lord, may the glory of this world continue to fade.

5th Divine Power

Divine power to destroy strongholds.
2 Corinthians 10.4

God is teaching and training me as I learn to rely on his divine power to destroy strongholds. The Lord is continuously attacking the enemy of my soul as he moves in to destroy the strongholds and citadels of Satan.

My training for reigning takes place amongst the skirmishes and battles in the prosecution of the victory of Christ.

As I fight from victory towards victory, I experience the divine power behind me as the Lord demolishes every stronghold that stands in his way.

Prayer: Lord, destroy the enemy strongholds that are in front of me.

6th Training for War

The Lord, my rock, who trains my hands for war.
Psalm 144.1

I am in combat school as I am continually in training for the spiritual battles ahead. The Lord uses the circumstances of my life to train me for combat with the enemy.

It's no good pretending that this life is ever going to be free from spiritual conflict and warfare. I cannot afford to be passive and therefore I have made myself available for combat training.

Day by day I am in God's boot camp as he is training my hands for war.

Prayer: Lord, train my hands for war.

7th Every Weapon

No weapon formed against me will prosper.
Isaiah 54.17

God has got my back as he protects me from the evil schemes and plots of an enemy who wants to destroy me and get me out of the way.

No weapon whatever form it takes will ultimately prosper against me if I remain under the protective covering of the blood of the Lamb.

As long as the blood of Jesus, our Passover Lamb, is on the doorposts of my life then I am under the protective shelter of God's almighty hand.

Prayer: Lord, thank you for the protection you give.

8th Fighting with Fruit

We are not waging war according to the flesh.
2 Corinthians 10.3

I have had to learn the hard way that you can't fight flesh with flesh and win. The only way to fight against the flesh and to win is with the fruit.

The spiritual weapons of prayer and the word are to be used against the enemy of our souls but when people are against us, we fight with the fruit.

Love trumps hate just as joy displaces sadness. Peace overcomes chaos and patience quietens tempers.

Kindness overwhelms a mean spirit and self-control wins over all the emotional strategies of the enemy.

Prayer: Lord, give me fruit for the fight.

9th Our Fight

Our fight is not against flesh and blood.
Ephesians 6.12

Many of the run-ins and conflicts that I experience in life are not what they seem. It's easy to miss or dismiss the fact that some of the major problems I encounter have been orchestrated by malevolent powers and unseen spiritual entities.

I have too often rejected this supernatural perspective but as I have had my eyes opened to see spiritual realities, I have learned to look beyond the people in front of me to the powers behind them who are manipulating their unwitting souls.

Prayer: Lord, help me to remember who the real enemy is.

10th The Difference

You have been raised with Christ.
Colossians 3.1

There is a vast difference between living on resurrection ground and living on natural ground. Living on resurrection ground means that my life is centred on God rather than on self.

This shift from a natural to a resurrection life involves keeping the Lord central in everything I do, think or say.

It means that in every situation of life I am constantly deferring to him and seeking his heart and mind.

It is of course a work of the Holy Spirit within as he teaches me and guides me in God's thoughts about everything.

Prayer: Lord, keep me living on a resurrection basis.

11th A Spiritual Church

A spiritual house.
1 Peter 2.5

The word church means an assembly or a mob! It is just a gathering of people and not even a religious one.

A spiritual church is centred around the life of the Holy Spirit who is living in the hearts and lives of the people who are gathered and drawn together by the Spirit of God.

It is not an organisation or an institution but a living organism. Its life and power come from within as the Holy Spirit moves within the hearts and lives of those he has called together.

Prayer: Lord, build your church.

12th Internalism not Externalism

You will receive power.
Acts 1.8

After the ascension of Jesus, his followers were waiting for something to happen. What they were looking for was something that was outside of themselves, something external.

They were looking for the restoration of the kingdom, perhaps a new political or social movement in which they had anticipated being key players.

But God began by doing something very different. Before anything else, his Spirit came into them and took hold of their lives so that they would become the instruments of his purpose.

It wasn't an external work it was internal, inside of them. Before anything took place externally it was all below the surface, in their hearts.

That is where the real work of God begins, not externally, but on the inside and then outward from there.

Prayer: Lord, keep doing your work inside me.

13th Forty Years

Forty years in the wilderness.
Deuteronomy 29.5

It has taken forty years in the wilderness for God to knock my self-sufficiency out of me. I have been humbled under the mighty hand of God as he has systematically stripped away much of my self-righteousness and the confidence that I once placed in my humanistic wisdom, schemes, plans and abilities.

A very old believer once said to me that it takes the Lord years to get us sufficiently emptied, weak and small so that we can bear His glory in our lives.

When he has me small enough and empty enough, then there is an opening for the Holy Spirit to work in glory.

Prayer: Lord, reveal your glory through my weakness.

14th Visible or Invisible

The fellowship of the Holy Spirit.
2 Corinthians 13.14

I have found the distinction between the visible and the invisible church to be really helpful as I try to locate myself within the visible church.

The visible church is what we see in buildings, denominations, ministers and the like. But the invisible church is less obvious and is located in the body of believers within whom the Spirit of the Lord is ruling and reigning.

The invisible church is not confined to particular denominations, religious systems or buildings.

It is found all over the world in the presence of the fellowship of the Holy Spirit.

Prayer: Lord, may I know the fellowship of the Holy Spirit.

15th Intuition

Perceiving in his spirit.
Mark 2.8

Intuition speaks of the tuition that the Holy Spirit is bringing to me as I walk with him. God speaks to me through my intuition as I come to know the things that he is communicating to me.

What I have learned is that my mind wants to filter or even veto what God is saying as my human ego working through my mind asserts its independence from God.

The Holy Spirit is my internal tutor who is always directing me if I am willing to listen and to do what he says, however offensive to my mind.

Prayer: Lord, help me to heed your intuition.

16th Breaking the Mould

Don't let the world around you squeeze you into its own mould.
Romans 12.2

The pressure is on me to be what the world wants me to be. It makes certain demands and has specific expectations about how I should conduct myself.

The world wants to make me what it needs me to be so that it can remain undisturbed and get on with its self-centred interests and preoccupations.

I no longer want to be pressured and squeezed in this way and I am praying for the strength to break the mould so that my life may be conformed to God's will rather than the will of worldly-minded people who want to get their own way.

Prayer: Lord, don't let me be squeezed into this world's mould.

17th Taken Captive

Taken captive to do his will.
2 Timothy 2.26

It is often perplexing when seemingly good people suddenly turn on us and become our enemies.

Hostility, conflict and aggressive behaviour overtake them as they assume an oppositional position and try to block our every move.

The explanation that we have from the apostles is that Satan takes God's people captive and has us doing the enemy's work.

The irony is that we can be deceived into thinking that we are doing God's will when in fact we are unwittingly doing the enemy's business.

Prayer: Lord, keep me from being taken captive by the enemy of my soul.

18th Don't Go There

Have nothing to do with them.
Ephesians 5.7

Radical separation unto God is at times a necessity for me. Bad company corrupts good character and I am cautious about getting drawn into unhelpful conversations or group thinking that is not honouring God.

There is a time to engage in the world but I can choose to stay away from certain people, places and things if I think that they will compromise my walk with God.

I know how easy it is to get contaminated by the world. Sin pollutes and it clings so I need to be antiseptic and staying clean means that I sometimes just don't go there.

Prayer: Lord, help me to know when not to go there.

19th The Communion of the Saints

Having the same love, being of one accord, of one mind.
Philippians 2.2

My life is dedicated to Christ and his people, the saints. I am deeply committed to the encouragement of the communion of saints at every opportunity.

The communion of saints is the spiritual union of the members of the Christian church both living and dead.

We are members of a mystical body of which Christ is the head.

Each member contributes to the good of all and shares in the welfare of all. This is very much more than just going to church or holding church services.

Prayer: Lord, help me to encourage the communion of saints.

20th Just Thinking

We have the mind of Christ.
1 Corinthians 2.16

The final frontier in my surrender to God is in the area of my thinking. I seem to want to cling tenaciously to my way of seeing and thinking about things.

Not so long ago someone said to me 'I don't think like that.' This comment challenged me because it made me realise that I have a choice about how I think.

These days I ask the Lord questions like how do you see this? What are you thinking about this person? Lord, how should we approach this situation?

I am continually searching for the Lord's mind on the circumstances that are in front of me. I am seeking an alignment of my thoughts with his. I am asking him to help me to see as he sees, to hear as he hears and to know as he knows.

Prayer: Lord, align my thinking with yours.

21st My House

As for me and my house, we will serve the Lord.
Joshua 24.15

Whatever anyone else is doing and no matter what they think, I have made a decision. That decision is for me and my household.

It is the decision to serve the Lord and it influences and informs every aspect of our lives. Nothing lies outside the scope of this commitment and it means that in our own family we live a different and distinctive life in this world.

Prayer: Lord, as for me and my house, we will serve you.

22ⁿᵈ His Lordship

Jesus is Lord.
1 Corinthians 12.3

The willingness to submit to the Lordship of Christ is the key to my spiritual life. Whenever I hit trouble, I look to see if I have rejected the Lordship of Christ, in that, or any other area of my life.

My biggest inner conflicts have been over the Lordship of Christ. The issue comes down to self-will which has taken back control and blocked me off from him.

Self-propulsion leads to trouble as my will leads me into wrong ways, wrong words and bad attitudes.

Prayer: Jesus, I submit to your Lordship.

23ʳᵈ Godly Sorrow

Godly Sorrow.
2 Corinthians 7.10

Saying sorry can be easy but Godly sorrow for sin is a much deeper thing. It has taken years for me to truly sense and feel the impact that my sin has had on others.

I feel genuine remorse and Godly sorrow for the damage I have done as well as the way that I have grieved God's heart.

My Godly sorrow goes well beyond saying sorry as I make living amends to those I have hurt and that includes God.

Prayer: Lord, I am sorry that I have grieved your heart and the hearts of many others.

24th The Will of Father

Whoever does the will of my father in heaven is my brother and sister.
Matthew 12.50

Jesus is saying that his relationship with me is linked to doing the will of his father in heaven. Doing the will of his father is central to having a family relationship with Jesus.

Even in Jesus' day many were following him and even claiming to believe but the reality and authenticity of their faith would only be revealed in their willingness to do the will of his father.

Belonging to a church family is a good thing but it is not to be confused with being Jesus' brother or sister. That relationship is confirmed as we do the will of his father.

Prayer: Jesus, may I do your father's will.

25th The Despised Things

Despised things of the world.
1 Corinthians 1.28

The world quests for self-glory, power, prestige, praise and honour. These manifestations of the desires of human pride seep into every corner of our lives and make demands on us to perform in various ways.

By way of contrast, the humility and meekness as demonstrated in the life of Jesus point toward a very different pathway in life.

Following Jesus takes us on a different course that involves things like looking foolish, being despised, looked down on, dismissed, ignored, overlooked, criticised, judged or falsely accused.

The purpose of this uncomfortable pathway is to extract our self-centred pride and ego. It is this way of humble access that I find myself on as I follow in the footsteps of my Lord.

Prayer: Lord, I choose to follow you rather than the approval of the world.

26th Keeping a Safe Distance

Therefore, come out from among them and be separate.
2 Corinthians 6.17

I have been brought up in what I now realise is a very compromised form of my faith. I have allowed my faith to become far too entwined, diluted and polluted by constant engagement and overly close contact with my culture.

This has allowed the values, attitudes, and behaviours of my surroundings to draw me further and further onto the world's ungodly turf with the result that my walk with God has been compromised.

I have discovered that the only way for me not to have my faith overrun and swamped by this world is to keep a degree of separation and distance from the culture.

I guess you could call it keeping a safe distance.

Prayer: Lord, help me to live at a safe distance from the world.

27th Religious Form

Holding the form of religion but denying its power.
2 Timothy 3.5

As I pursue a real and deep relationship with the Lord, I find myself in conflict with some of the outward forms of my religion that seem to deny the power and presence of God.

I find myself being pressed, pressured and compromised into participating in forms of worship where it feels to me like God is being left out and excluded.

These forms of religion can look very impressive from a worldly point of view but what if it's not the real thing? What if it's an imitation or a fake?

If it is merely an outward thing it will lack the spiritual power to bring life, as well as the deep and lasting change that I am looking for.

Prayer: Lord, may I not exchange power for form.

28th Renewal of My Mind

Be transformed by the renewal of your mind.
Romans 12.2

My mind is a powerful tool and therefore it needs to be in a safe pair of hands. Under the supervision and direction of the Spirit of God, my mind is under good government that has a positive and transformative effect on my life.

However, if my self-centred ego, driven by the energy of my soul, is allowed to dominate my mind, it is then that my thinking can lead me astray.

Transformation and positive change can take place when my mind is being renewed and my thinking is being directed by the Holy Spirit from within.

Prayer: Lord, renew my mind and my thinking.

29th Secret and Shameful Ways

We have renounced secret and shameful ways we do not use deception.
2 Corinthians 4.2

This straightforward and honest approach to life is a distinguishing feature of a life lived in fellowship with the Lord.

There is an intentional renunciation of all forms of secrecy and deception.

This is a walk in the light and that means absolute honesty in all my dealings both with myself and with others.

Plotting, scheming, and secret agendas are not the right tools for the Kingdom of God.

For those of us who have been schooled in these ways, it means a conscious and continuous attentiveness to the Spirit of the Lord who blows the whistle on this type of behaviour, usually at the earliest stage.

Prayer: Lord, blow the whistle on any secrecy and deception in my life.

30th Resurrection Ground

The old has gone and the new has come.
2 Corinthians 5.17

God only builds on the new foundations that he lays when he places his Spirit within us and gives us a new beginning.

Our old selves before the waters of baptism into Christs' death are of no use to God. He is not trying to reform the old nature instead he has finished it off on the cross.

God only builds on resurrection ground and the foundation stone that has been laid on that ground is Christ. The old has gone and the new has come.

Prayer: Lord, build my life on resurrection ground.

July

1st Eagles Wings

They will rise up with wings like eagles.
Isaiah 40.31

The wind of the Spirit comes to raise me up. The thermals of the Lord's breath provide the lift that I need.

As with the eagle the lift is not achieved through frantic flapping but through waiting for the thermals and then trusting the wind to do the work.

God's Spirit raises my spirit as I rely on his power to lift me higher, both up and away from the forces of spiritual gravity that are seeking to pull me down from my ascended position in Christ.

Prayer: Lord, lift me higher in the heavenly places into Christ Jesus.

2nd Alive to God

Reckon yourself dead to sin but alive to God.
Romans 6.11

I reckon myself dead to sin when I decide not to invest in my old nature. I ignore it and treat it as if it is extinct.

Instead of focusing on the former domination and control of my old self, I assign it to the graveyard and then I concentrate on living my life in union with Christ.

I refuse to live in the old ways and former habits of my old nature and I constantly remind myself that I am no longer the same person that I was before Christ.

My old self died with Christ and my new self has been raised with him. I keep doing the maths, I reckon myself alive to God but dead to sin and it works out fine.

Prayer: Lord, help me to stay dead to sin and alive to you.

3rd Inward Renewal

Outwardly we are wasting away, yet inwardly we are being renewed day by day.
2 Corinthians 4.16

There is a wonderful paradox in the spiritual life and it concerns the relationship between our bodies and our spirits.

Just as our bodies, age and mileage start to show in different ways, this decline is matched with a corresponding increase in our spiritual vigour and life.

Day by day I experience renewal and an ongoing regeneration in my spirit which has an invigorating effect on the rest of my being.

I am more aware than ever that I am not my body and that one day I will be able to trade it in when it is no longer fit for purpose.

Prayer: Lord, thank you for your daily inward renewal of my spirit.

4th Losing Sensitivity

Having lost all sensitivity.
Ephesians 4.19

Losing or not having a sensitivity to the Spirit of the Lord has serious consequences. This is because our hearts are being formed in two ways.

Either they are being softened by the Holy Spirit as we come into alignment with him or our hearts are becoming increasingly hardened as we reject his overtures towards us.

If we continually incline ourselves away from him and we don't want to see him or hear him, then God gives us over to our desire, so that as our hearts grow harder, we lose the capacity to know the Lord.

Prayer: Lord, incline my heart towards you.

5th Desperate Enough

Jesus, son of David, have mercy on me.
Luke 18.38

There is nothing like the gift of desperation to bring us to God. Sometimes the best thing that can happen is for everything to fall apart.

When all around us seems to be failing or going wrong it is then that my heart has a choice. Am I going to blame God and try to sort it all out myself or am I going to humble myself, admit my mistakes and ask him to show me his way through?

Prayer: Lord, thank you for the gift of desperation.

6th No House Sharing

The train of his robe filled the temple.
Isaiah 6.1

God does not co-occupy his houses he wants to fill them. What was true of the Old Testament temple is true for my life as a disciple of Jesus.

God will not share me with anyone or anything, he wants every part of my life, all of it. He wants the whole house, not just rooms.

It is only as I hand over the keys to the house of my life that he can come in and take possession of it.

It is his presence within that fills my spiritual house with glory. It is not my glory but his glory as he resides within my heart.

Prayer: Lord, fill this temple of my life with your glory.

7th All My Fountains

All my fountains are in you.
Psalm 87.7

I want all my fountains to be in the Lord. I am no longer looking for other streams and sources of life apart from the life of God in Christ.

He is my only source and he is my only river. I am praying for rivers of living water to flow from within my heart.

I am asking the Lord for a constant supply of the freshwater of the Spirit to flow through me to purify my heart and give me life.

Without water, I will die physically but without the water of life, I will wither and die spiritually.

Prayer: Lord, give me this water to drink.

8th Another Comforter

Another Comforter.
John 14.16

The Holy Spirit is not an impersonal force or power. He is a person who Jesus described as the counsellor or helper and intercessor who would be with us and in us.

It is his influence and spiritual presence within me that enables me to live the life that Jesus is calling me to live.

It is this inner witness of the Spirit that is the source of my spiritual life and it is his power that is at work within me.

I am increasingly attentive to his direction and these days I try not to ignore or override his humble and subtle promptings.

He generally doesn't shout, but his quiet promptings I must not disobey. I am learning that his counsel is much wiser than my best thinking or reason.

Prayer: Holy Spirit, help me to know you better.

9th On Track

A highway shall be there, and it shall be called the Way of Holiness.
Isaiah 35.8

It is so exciting to be on track with God. To have the awareness that I am on the path that I was always meant to be on.

Over the years so many things have pulled me off course and held me captive. But now I am free to pursue the Lord in what is proving to be a wonderful and exciting journey of discovery.

This is what I always wanted but so many things have blocked me off and diverted me from living in dynamic fellowship with the Holy Spirit.

Prayer: Lord, keep me on your high paths.

10th Spiritual Faculties

The blind will see and those who see will become blind.
John 9.39

The spiritual faculties that I received in embryonic form when my eyes were first opened by the Lord have faced repeated and sustained attacks from the enemy.

Few and far between are those who have been able to give me instruction in the development of these faculties.

It is only now, many years later that I have found the instruction and help that I need to develop my latent spiritual senses and finally to grow in the deeper things of God.

Prayer: Lord, thank you for the gift of spiritual sight.

11th Supernatural Battle

Spiritual forces.
Ephesians 6.12

Spiritual enlightenment is supernatural and so is spiritual blindness. I now regard my spiritual enlightenment as a miracle.

It was a battle to break through the spiritual blindness that I was living in and as I look back, I can see that there was an enormous spiritual battle for control of my soul.

Spiritual conflict continues as the Lord seeks to bring me further into the light through the impartation of more revelation.

As God is broadening my spiritual horizons the enemy and his spiritual forces are doing everything they can, to block my increasing spiritual enlightenment.

Prayer: Lord, give me victory over the enemy.

12th Discovery and Wonder

Living and active.
Hebrews 4.12

The question on my mind is what is God going to do today? Where is the Spirit moving? What is he saying? What does he want me to see?

This life in the Spirit is full of wonder and discovery as I move out into this world where God is at work.

It's his work and he is offering me the opportunity to join him. It is full of wonder and there are many surprises in store as each day God reveals his hand and his heart towards the people around me.

Prayer: Lord, help me to see your hand, to know your heart and to join you in what you are doing.

13th The Adventure

Come follow me.
Matthew 4.19

Following Jesus is a lifelong adventure. It's a never-ending voyage of discovery and delight. Every day there are new things to see and fresh discoveries to be made.

It's a brilliant way of life as there is never a dull day.

Of course, it's not an easy life because it requires acting against one's self and sacrificing immediate gratification for long-term growth.

Above all this way of life is fun, filled with joy and a wonderful sense of inner freedom that is just not available anywhere else.

It is priceless.

Prayer: Lord, keep me in this adventure of faith.

14th The Quest

I am a sojourner on the earth.
Psalm 119.19

My journey deeper into Christ is a quest. A quest is a long search for something that is difficult to find. It is a journey towards a specific mission or goal.

Within my heart is a God-given desire to go further and to move on in this journey into Him. I can never sit back on my laurels for long because there is one who is calling me up higher.

There is always new territory in the Spirit to be discovered and explored. I cannot set up camp for long as I am being propelled forward and onward.

Prayer: Lord, keep me moving forward with you.

15th This is That

This is that which was spoken.
Acts 2.16

Some of the snares that I have had to unhook from are the ideas that I have formed in my mind about how things should be.

For years I prayed for the spirit of wisdom and revelation not realising that I already possessed it and not knowing that I was experiencing it.

I would see things in the scripture and comprehend spiritual realities but what I didn't realise was the connection between what I was experiencing and the scriptures.

In my case, this experience of spiritual seeing was the same thing that is prayed for in the Ephesian church.

I just had not been able to see the connection. Now as I walk through life, I am making constant connections between the scriptures and my experience of life.

Every day I am saying 'oh this is that!'

Prayer: Lord, connect my life with your word.

16th Resilience

Your mighty strength that you exerted in Christ.
Ephesians 1.20

Through the often difficult and sometimes disturbing circumstances of my life, God has been building resilience in me. What this means is that he gives me the necessary strength to meet the next calamity or problem.

It is not the strength of my flesh but the power of his Spirit within who rises up to meet the adversity in front of me.

Life is God's training camp and there are lessons to be learned in any and every circumstance of life no matter how seemingly difficult.

The evidence of this resilience is in the peace and rest in God that I experience even in the most troubling of events.

Prayer: Lord, give me your strength and build my resilience.

17th Breaking

A broken and contrite heart.
Psalm 51.17

God has had to break me to reveal my self-sufficiency, pride, independence and rebellion.

Through some very difficult times and deep personal struggles, he has brought to the surface many of my hidden faults that I would otherwise have been unaware of.

This is not something that I would have elected to do but it has meant that the life I live now is so much better than the old one where I was carrying around a lot of unwanted baggage in the form of character defects and blind spots.

Prayer: Lord, continue to break me of my sin.

18th The Rest Laboratory

Make every effort to enter that rest.
Hebrews 4.11

I feel like my life is one long experiment in the practice of rest. By this, I mean that every circumstance, situation and problem of life is an experiment and laboratory test to see how my peace and rest in God holds out.

It is very cool to discover God's rest in the middle of life's chaos. It's like standing in the eye of the storm in perfect peace whilst all around is turmoil and noise.

This awareness of God's rest has given me a new 'bring it on' attitude to life and life's problems.

Each one is an opportunity for me to practice the rest of God. These days I am looking to operate from a place of rest in all the circumstances of life.

That's the challenge and I'm up for it.

Prayer: Lord, keep me in your rest.

19th Impartation

I have come that you may have life.
John 10.10

Having received the gift of God's uncreated life, his Zoe, I have an intense desire to see others share in it.

I carry a message which has life attached to it. It is a living thing and I want others to catch it too because it is so wonderful and I don't want them to go without it.

The question is how can this life of God that I am experiencing be imparted to another person? The answer is that only God can do this work of transmission and impartation.

We can pass on information but the impartation of his life through us is a supernatural process that only he can do.

Prayer: Lord, impart your life through my life.

20th Piggy Backing

Infants in Christ.
1 Corinthians 3.1

I am aware that people piggyback off my faith. They lean on my faith, my teaching and my encouragement to help themselves to keep going on with the Lord.

This may be alright at the beginning but it is not something that works in the long term, for whilst there will be times when we need to rely on the faith of others, it is important to develop our faith so that we can stand on our own two feet, spiritually.

Each of us needs a faith and a walk with God that is independent of anyone or anything else.

The faith of those around us is important and encouraging but we all need to be self-starters in the sense that we don't need others to get us up and running.

Prayer: Lord, help me to stand on my own faith in you.

21st Carnality

People of the flesh.
1 Corinthians 3.1

Carnality brings the natural into the realm of the spiritual and if I make it the governing thing in my life then the result will be that it closes down the spiritual.

For me, spirituality involves continually moving off natural ground and intentionally moving into the realm of the Spirit.

The depth and quality of my spirituality are determined by how far I am willing to allow the Spirit to take me off natural ground and onto spiritual ground.

Prayer: Lord, keep moving me off natural ground and onto spiritual ground.

22nd What God Has Prepared

What God has prepared for those who love him.
1 Corinthians 2.9

It is difficult to set our thoughts beyond this life particularly as this world tends to become all-absorbing.

This makes it all the more important that I contemplate my future life and live today in the consciousness of my future in the new earth that is to come.

God has prepared a future for me that is beyond my comprehension and there is work to do for me to be properly prepared for it.

What I do know and what I can comprehend by faith is that it is going to be good, very good, and for that, I am continually thankful.

Prayer: Lord, thank you that I have a wonderful future with your son.

23rd What I am Here For

To be adopted.
Ephesians 1.5

The emphasis of most of the spiritual teaching that I have received has been on salvation. Its core message has been about escaping and being saved from the negative judgment of my righteous and loving God.

What I have not received so much instruction about is the question of what I have been saved for. It is only now that I have been discovering the importance of knowing what I have been saved for.

I have been shown that I have been saved for a purpose and that my earthly life is being directed by God so that by the time my earthly life is over God will have shaped me into a mature son ready for my adoption in the new heaven and the new earth.

Prayer: Lord, may I always remember what I am here for.

24th Ruling and Reigning with Him

We will also reign with him.
2 Timothy 2.12

The goal of God's program for my life is that my relationship with him and my life lived in union with Christ will enable him to entrust me with my inheritance in the life of the world to come.

One aspect of this inheritance will be the position that the Lord will allocate to me based on the life that I have lived and the relationship that I have with him here on earth.

I once knew an old Christian who used to call the time that we have here on earth our 'training for reigning.'

God wants us to be mature rulers in his new creation. People who know him, do his will and are already familiar with and trained in his ways.

Prayer: Lord, train me for reigning.

25th Imperishable Inheritance

An inheritance that can never perish, spoil or fade.
1 peter 1.3-4

Anyone blessed enough to receive an inheritance in this life will know what a responsibility it is to keep it and not to have it eroded by inflation and tax or just stolen in some way or another.

Whatever my inheritance in Christ will be I know that it will not be diminished or taken away. I have God's guarantee that I will receive everything that he has promised me and more because he always gives a full and overflowing measure.

Prayer: Lord, thank you for my inheritance in heaven.

26th The Eternal Purpose of God

The world to come.
Hebrews 2.5

The position of the dominion of the church over the world in the ages to come is a challenging thing to consider.

Hebrews tells us that it is not to the angels that God has subjected the earth to but to the Son, that is Christ, and then to the rest of the sons in Christ, that is the believers.

This is what God is saying when he promises to bring many sons to glory. He is promising to bring us as coheirs in our union with Christ into the position of dominion over the inhabited earth in the age to come.

That is the eternal purpose of God.

Prayer: Lord, help me to embrace your eternal purpose in my life.

27th Oblivious

They think it strange.
1 Peter 4.4

I am surrounded by many loving and caring people who live good lives in a natural sense. The remarkable thing is that on the whole, they are completely oblivious to the realities of God and life in the Spirit.

Life for them is lived solely on a material basis with very little attention, if any, paid to the spiritual dimension of life in this world.

Their life is one of spiritual blindness as they cannot perceive the things of God. It's a life of not knowing and it is normalised so that life in the Spirit seems strange, weird or dull in comparison to a materialistic way of living.

Prayer: Lord, open the blind eyes around me.

28th Exodus

To bring them out of that land.
Exodus 3.8

I have got to a point in my life where God is calling me out. Out from the life that I have been living and into new territory with Him.

My Exodus involves leaving behind a familiar place in God and moving into a new and unfamiliar place of dependence and willing obedience rather than self-rule.

It's a further pressing into the Spirit and another step in my ongoing surrender to the government of God in every aspect of my life.

Exodus involves leaving everything behind that is either a hindrance or not useful for my future life with God.

It's a renunciation of my former life that was lived in the old country of self-determinism and independence from God's dynamic reign within me.

Prayer: Lord, help me to leave behind everything that is not of you.

29th Collapse

The present form of this world is passing away.
1 Corinthians 7.31

In the old hymn 'abide with me' there is a verse which says 'change and decay in all around I see.' It is a bit gloomy but it is true of life in this world.

Structures are prone to collapse and this is the case with so many things including our human bodies.

The medical world is constantly researching and working hard to find ways to keep our bodies from collapsing because the whole tendency of our frail form is in that direction.

Other structures such as big businesses and even churches need a lot of effort and soul force to keep them away from their tendency to collapse.

God's answer is not found in this world but in the life of the world to come at the renewal of all things.

The people in the wilderness experienced a foretaste of this as for forty years their clothes and sandals did not wear out.

We too experience foretastes of this when God steps into a seemingly hopeless situation of collapse and brings about a renewal that no amount of work on our part could have brought about.

Prayer: Lord, renew me and keep me from collapse.

30th Incorruptible Crowns

We have an incorruptible crown of rejoicing.
1 Corinthians 9.25

Athletes of old were rewarded for their victory with wreaths made of laurel and other perishable plants and flowers.

Like their victory, the crown of rejoicing would fade and die away but the crown of the victorious Christ will never perish, spoil or fade.

My crown in union with Christ is incorruptible, immortal and will last forever. It is part of my glorious inheritance that awaits me when all things will be revealed including my true identity as a son of God and a co-heir with Christ as he reigns in his kingdom.

Prayer: Lord, crown me with rejoicing.

31st The Source

The Lord evaluates the motives.
Proverbs 21.2

It is so important to examine the source of things. In spiritual matters, the origin of things is of great significance and importance.

In seeking to find the source, I ask myself questions. Is this idea that I am being presented with from God or has it been conceived in the human mind?

Has the Spirit of God given birth to this?

Is the source of this found in soul-power or Spirit-power?

Ideas birthed in soul power are often pleasing to the mind and the aspirations of many but once acted on they lack the life and power of God behind them.

Prayer Lord, help me to discern the source.

August

1st Knowing His Ways

They have not known my ways.
Hebrews 3.10

It has taken a good proportion of my life to start to get to know God's ways. I have been well-schooled in the ways of the world but I now have an intense desire to discover more about the ways of God.

The reason that I have been so slow to learn God's ways is largely down to the waywardness of my heart. My old nature and this world have their ideas about how things should be done and these old ways are often not God's way.

I am now beginning to learn how he likes things done and since then, life has taken on a new sense of discovery and adventure as I have enrolled in the school of the Spirit.

Prayer: Lord, teach me your ways.

2nd Lord of My Opinions

How long will you go on limping between two opinions?
1 Kings 18.21

Enthroning Christ as the Lord of my life means that all my opinions, likes, dislikes, beliefs, and thinking come under his jurisdiction. I am no longer a free thinker because I am now submitting all my thoughts to his authority.

It is not my opinion or anyone else's that matters most to me. Jesus is now ruling my life and it is his opinion that is the most important thing.

He is moving me off my self-centred position, taking me off the throne, and enabling me to take my proper position under his rightful authority.

All my other lords are being challenged as one by one they are dethroned. It is a great liberation to let go of ways of thinking and opinions that have damaged my life in the past.

Prayer: Lord, help me to go with your opinion.

3rd Lord of My Life

None of you can be my disciple unless you give up everything you have.
Luke 14.33

Lord of my eyes, my gaze and my looking. Lord of my seeing and my perception. Lord of my heart and its desires.

Lord of my tongue and its words. Lord of my dreams and my imagination. Lord of my past, my present and my future.

Lord of my ears and my hearing. Lord of the years that are remaining. Lord of my time. Lord of my work. Lord of my possessions.

Lord of my body and all its parts and functions. Lord of my old and new nature. Lord of my attitudes, moods, reactions and responses.

Lord of my gifts. Lord of my character and appearance. Lord in the small things as well as the larger things.

Lord of all my decisions.

Prayer: Lord, may you be the Lord of everything in my life.

4th Is This It?

The light of the knowledge of God.
2 Corinthians 4.6

I am so thankful that the Lord put within me a Godly sense of dissatisfaction with life as it is. I was spiritually blind but I didn't know it. I had just an inkling that there must be more to life than this.

Materialistic pursuits such as jobs, money, status and leisure did not do it for me. They could not deliver what I was searching for deep down in my heart.

I felt lost and trapped in confusion and I couldn't find a way out. The answer to my longing and my many questions came as God began to reveal himself to me in the face of Jesus Christ.

Prayer: Lord Jesus, thank you for bringing me out of spiritual confusion.

5th God in the Heart

For it is God who works in you.
Philippians 2.13

A while ago I was asked a simple question. The question was this: what is God doing in your heart?

At the time I had no idea what God was doing in my heart and my honest reply was that I didn't know.

The reason I didn't know was that I was not aware that it was possible for me to have a real moment-by-moment relationship with God.

Things are different now as I am much more aware of God's presence in me by his Spirit and his continuous dealings with me in my heart.

Prayer: Lord, raise my awareness of you in my heart.

6th New Frontiers in God

They were looking for a better country.
Hebrews 11.16

I enjoy going to new and different places but for me, the most exciting journey is the inner one.

Knowing God through his inner working in my heart is the great new frontier. It is the most wonderful journey of discovery and the expedition of a lifetime. This is the place of my pioneering on the never-ending journey of discovery into the centre of the heart of God.

It is the coalface of mission in this world. As I dig here everything else takes shape from this gold mine of the Spirit.

Prayer: Lord, take me to new frontiers in you.

7th A Great Tragedy

I never knew you.
Matthew 7.23

The great tragedy that surrounds me every day is found in all the people who just don't know my Lord.

All around me are people who have no connection with God or any consciousness of his existence.

The people I mix with are good people on a natural plane but what they lack is the most important and valuable thing in the world, a living and real relationship with God.

This is a great tragedy.

Prayer: Lord, have mercy.

8th Absolute Dependence

Apart from me, you can do nothing.
John 15.5

I am increasingly being moved by the Lord into a position of absolute dependence on the Holy Spirit.

The independent thinking and pattern of living that I was schooled in have given way to a new way of thinking and living.

These have been given in Christ through the work of his Spirit within me. Absolute dependence on the Holy Spirit is the way forward in this wonderful school of the Spirit.

Prayer: Holy Spirit, teach me to depend on you absolutely.

9th Many Such Things

And many such things you do.
Matthew 7.13

Religiousness is not necessarily a sign of faith and I have found it to be a pitfall in my walk with God.

My religiousness manifested itself in furious activity for God that looked like genuine faith but wasn't.

This religiousness was a cover for the fact that I had lost my connection with God through poor decisions based on self and over-exposure to traditional, lifeless, formal, and legalistic religion.

I am no longer willing to sacrifice my intimacy with the Holy Spirit to the demands of religiousness and the spirit of deception that can so easily hide behind it.

Prayer: Holy Spirit, remove any religiousness that blocks your life in me.

10th Hunger and Fullness

In him, all the fullness of God was pleased to dwell.
Colossians 1.19

I am very hungry for God. I have been praying 'Holy Spirit I am hungry for you.' I am praying for the fullness of God that will satisfy this intense appetite that I have for his Holy Spirit.

I am asking, seeking and knocking for more of the fullness of the Holy Spirit.

I don't feel that I can go on without more of the Holy Spirit in my life.

I need the manna in the wilderness and the bread that comes down from heaven to feed my hungry heart.

Prayer: Holy Spirit, I am hungry for you.

11th Revive Thy Work

Revive thy work.
Habakkuk 3.2

I am praying that the Lord will renew what I have seen in the past and that he will refresh those experiences of his presence and power.

I am asking the Lord for a renewed acceleration in the life of his Spirit and a rediscovery of his invigorating power that makes all things new.

Prayer: Lord, revive your work in me.

12th More Revelation

To reveal his son in me.
Galatians 1.16

I am praying to God for more revelation of His Son Jesus Christ in me.

The great Apostle to the gentiles spoke about how important this revelation was to him. He showed how God had revealed Christ in him so that he might preach him. He knew the importance of knowing the revelation of Christ inside of him.

I am aware that the revelation of Christ in me is a mystical thing and at present, it is something that I have only fragmentary knowledge of.

I am not sure exactly what the answer to this prayer will bring forth in my experience but whatever form it takes it will be more than I know at present and that will be good.

Prayer: Lord, reveal your son in me.

13th Faithlessness

Lest we drift away.
Hebrews 2.1

Hitting up against faithlessness in the church is a very disconcerting experience. How is it possible to spend your whole life involved in the church but to have a high level of faithlessness?

Faithlessness can be contagious and it is all too easy to fall into a lifestyle that requires very little active faith in God.

In such an atmosphere of unbelief, it is much easier to slowly drift away and lose the zest and joy that comes from a daily faith life and active walk with the Lord.

Prayer: Lord, keep me in faith.

14th Carrying the Presence

If your presence does not go with me.
Exodus 33.15

Israel was conscious of the fact that they carried God's presence wherever they went; this was symbolised in the Ark of the covenant which went with them wherever their feet trod.

In this dispensation, the presence of God is carried by believers in Christ within whom His presence resides by His Spirit.

I seek to be one of those believers who is a carrier of God's powerful presence to the people around me.

Prayer: Lord, may I carry your presence.

15th Excluding Him

They received him not.
John 1.11

There is a deliberate strategy of the enemy to exclude every person and every situation of life from the influence of God's Son Jesus.

All around the world Jesus Christ is being excluded as moment by moment he is pushed aside by humanly inspired ways of thinking and living.

There is an intentional, hidden, and relentless campaign of exclusion taking place as the light of Christ is being shut out and people's eyes blinded to his divine reality.

Prayer: Lord let your light shine in the darkness of this world.

16th Distracted

Martha was distracted.
Luke 10.40

One of the tactics of the enemy is to keep me busy. It is very important to him that I am kept preoccupied so that I don't have any time each day to be with my Lord.

These preoccupations can be good and worthwhile things but they can have the effect of keeping me distracted and far too busy to attend to God's thoughts and directions for my life.

Even when I intentionally seek to listen to God, I am often met with a series of distracting thoughts or urgent external interruptions that either break the flow of my time with the Lord or just prevent that time of fellowship from happening in the first place.

Knowing the battle that is on with distraction, I am training myself to close my ears to this world with its constant noise and instead to make time to open myself up to the world of the Spirit of God where my mind is intentionally preoccupied with the Lord.

Prayer: Lord, help me not to be too busy for you.

17th Everything is Broken

Falling Short.
Romans 3.23

Everything in this world is to some extent broken. As a result of 'the fall', we live in a 'gone wrong' world where things easily fail or fall apart.

Our bodies, our minds, our machines, as well as our systems and organisations are all apt to malfunction in some way or another.

Even our relationships are prone to break down at every level from marriage to international relations.

God's answer was not to remake this world but to start a new one and he has invited us to populate it.

Entry into the new earth is through the cross of Christ as we exchange our broken natures for his new one.

Remembering and accepting that this is a broken world goes a long way towards living with all the brokenness that I encounter around me as well as in myself.

Prayer: Lord, help me to live well as a broken person in this broken world.

18th Recognition

He made himself of no reputation.
Philippians 2.7

The great temptation is to use whatever platform the Lord has given us to gain personal recognition and worldly praise.

The Pharisees liked to be recognised in the market places and they loved the limelight provided by their religious status and apparel.

I am not immune from this inner need for personal recognition through my religious position as my ego is always ready to claim its right to be recognised.

Obscurity, anonymity and hiddenness marked much of the life of Jesus and I seek to follow him in this way.

Prayer: Lord, I seek your recognition alone.

19th Absolute Lordship

Jesus is Lord.
Romans 10.9

The absolute Lordship of Jesus Christ is the key to my fellowship with him and my life of usefulness in this world.

This has been the main battleground in my spiritual life as I have argued with him and fought with him over the things that I have wanted to hold onto and that he has said must go.

My lords have been many as my self-life has tenaciously clung onto its commitment to self-rule.

Step by step God has used the circumstances of my life to break down these other lords as he moves me increasingly into the place of His absolute Lordship which is the place of true freedom in Christ.

Prayer: Lord, may you have absolute Lordship in my life.

20th The God Who Speaks

Dumb idols.
1 Corinthians 12.2

My God is not a dumb idol because he speaks to me through the Bible. When I read it, God's word comes alive to me and through it, he communicates with me.

God also speaks to me in the inner man of my spirit. In this way, I receive instruction, guidance, encouragement and warnings. He reassures me and communicates his loving presence to me. It is direct communication from God and I never want to be without it.

God is not dumb because he is still speaking to his people and that includes me.

Prayer: Lord, open my ears to hear you.

21st Without Holiness

Without holiness, no one will see the Lord.
Hebrews 12.14

There are no shortcuts or easier options with God. No amount of religious activity or external devotion can be a substitute for a heart that is set apart unto the Lord.

Holiness manifests in lifestyle and outward behaviour but it doesn't start there. Holiness begins with the dedication and separation of my heart to God.

Holiness is the dethronement of self and the enthroned of the Lord in my heart at all times and in all places.

Prayer: Lord, I want to be holy.

22nd Denying Self

He must deny himself.
Matthew 16.24

The litmus test of my discipleship is found in the question how much of self is in this? Is what I am doing in this act of service done in the power of the Spirit or am I only leaning on my own personal power, knowledge and experience?

I need to ask myself how much am I pushing this or forcing it and trying to get a result through my power.

This is very subtle as my 'self' doesn't like playing second fiddle through being denied and it wants to exercise its power as well as to take the credit.

The self-denial that Jesus is teaching cuts deep into all my activities with the sharp knife of the truth. It asks the awkward question about how much of what I am doing is just me operating under my own steam and in my strength rather than moving in the power of God.

Self-denial involves my continual refusal to rely on myself and an intentional decision to trust in the Lord.

Prayer: Lord, teach me to rely on your power and wisdom.

23rd Life to the Body

He who raised Jesus from the dead will also give life to your mortal bodies.
Romans 8.11

There is health that comes from a life lived in communion with God. Living life God's way leads us into patterns and rhythms of life that are wholesome and good.

Whilst none of us is immune to illness or attacks on our health there is a provision for health and strength through the Spirit of God as he works within us.

The resurrection power of God is at work in us and I am increasingly aware of the strengthening of body and mind that is taking place in me as my spirit feeds on the life of God's Spirit within.

Prayer: Lord, strengthen me in body and mind through your Spirit.

24th A Sabbath Rest

I will give you rest.
Matthew 11.28

I take a sabbath day of rest every week. On this day I intentionally distance myself from my work and practice rest.

Rest doesn't mean that I do nothing but what it does mean is that I set aside all the uncertainty, difficulty and fretful worry surrounding my work.

My sabbath is often not an easy day as I wrestle with letting go of my self-importance that tells me that the work will collapse without my immediate input.

The fruit of my sabbath rest is that when I return to work, I find that I am operating from a place of rest and calm rather than anxiety and fretting.

Prayer: Lord Jesus, I come to you for rest.

25th Pleasing Father

I always do those things that please him.
John 8.29

I am living my life not to please myself but for the pleasure of my Heavenly Father. I don't want to serve him as a reluctant slave but as a willing son.

I want my life to be a joy and a delight to him. I don't want to be a grudging, grumpy, reluctant or rebellious son.

Instead, I want to be enthusiastic, wholehearted, eager, willing, obedient and joyful in my sonship.

Prayer: Father, I want my life to bring you joy.

26th Christ in Everything

He who fills everything in every way.
Ephesians 1.23

It is good to continually remind myself that everything that is not of Christ will be removed. He is going to fill everything in every way so that nothing which is not of him will remain.

Christ will be in and through everything in a way that is almost totally beyond my comprehension.

Here and now, he is already in me as he is expanding and increasing his territory within my life.

Everything in me that is not of him will ultimately be removed and only what is of him will remain.

Prayer: Jesus, fill every part of me with your life.

27th Apart from Me

Apart from me, you can do nothing.
John 15.5

I can do a lot. I can exhaust myself in doing things for God. I can plan and work and toil every hour of the day and night in the service of my God.

However, despite all this effort, the spiritual value of it all may be zero. It is not what is done for God that will last but what is done by him.

The true spiritual value of my efforts can only be measured by the extent to which they have been initiated and promoted by God.

The question for me is not how much work have I done for the Lord but how much of him is in it.

That's the only thing that matters because it is only what is done in him and from him, that will last.

Prayer: Lord, apart from you I can do nothing.

28th Tarry

Tarry ye in Jerusalem.
Luke 24.49

At his ascension, Jesus instructed the disciples to tarry in Jerusalem until they were endued with power from on high.

The disciples had been in the ministry with Jesus for three years and they knew a lot. They had absorbed his teaching and his practice of ministry but their training was not enough.

What they needed was the power of the Holy Spirit to bring them to life so that the life of Jesus would become manifest in them.

The instruction they were given was to wait and not to try to do anything until they received the power and the wisdom of the Lord.

Prayer: Lord, help me tarry before rushing ahead.

29th Not I But Christ

Not I but Christ.
Galatians 2.20

The denial of ego is summed up in words 'not I.' Ego is the promotion of myself by myself. It is the root of all my problems.

Ever since the fall, it has been persuading us that God is holding things back from us and that we need to grasp them for ourselves.

Ungoverned my ego wants to dominate, manipulate and control to get its way because it must get what it wants.

The key to breaking the destructive power of my ego is in the words 'but Christ.'

As Christ takes charge and gets to work within me, he continually challenges my egotistical beliefs, attitudes and behaviours to bring me to a place of humble dependence on his goodwill for my life rather than being at the mercy of my ego drives.

Prayer: Lord Jesus, break my ego and live in me.

30th I in Him

I in Him.
John 15.5

Christ in me. He is the powerhouse and source of everything of eternal value in my life. Without him in me I have nothing and I am nothing.

He is my everything and my all in all. Without him, I can do nothing and everything I do without him is of no lasting value.

He is alive in me and it is his life that gives me life.

Prayer: Jesus, increase your life in me.

31st Like God

You will be like God.
Genesis 3.5

This was the big temptation at the beginning and it's still with us every day. Am I going to claim powers and abilities that are in truth beyond my power and ability? Am I going to plan, scheme or even boast of things that are beyond my human reach?

I am no longer trying to do anything without God or beyond the bounds of what he has called me to do.

This is very frustrating for the doers around me who want to use their considerable soul force and human ability to get things done in their human power and strength.

Prayer: Lord, help me not to move outside your will.

September

1st Resisters

You always resist the Holy Spirit.
Acts 7.51

There are so many ways to resist and reject God but religious resistance to God is the most subtle and deceptive of all.

Instead of obeying God it creates its system of self-justification and gets very busy with all sorts of work for God.

It looks like God's work and it may well gain recognition as such in the community but if it is just an expression of self-will and ego-driven determination then it may be no more than a manifestation of the rejection of God's will and God's way.

However noble, if my independent and headstrong way is just an expression of my self-determination it will always be a manifestation of my resistance to God and his will at depth.

Prayer: Lord, may I respond to your will and not resist it.

2nd Exactly

I do exactly what my father has commanded me.
John 14.31

A lot hinges on this word exactly. It doesn't say roughly or vaguely but exactly. What I have learned is that when it comes to doing the will of my Father, I need to be attentive to his precise instructions.

I have learned the importance of following his directions and instructions very closely. God knows when and how he wants things done and I know the importance and the joy of doing things exactly the way he wants them.

Prayer: Lord, help me to do things exactly the way you want them.

3rd Moving by the Spirit

Moved by the Spirit, he went.
Luke 2.27

Living and moving in the Spirit is a wonderful thing. When it happens, you know that the Holy Spirit is urging you and directing your every move. You find that you are just where he wants you to be. You know that you are there with the message or the deed that is needed at that moment.

Having my life timed and overseen by the Holy Spirit is an amazing experience as I find myself in situations which have been prearranged by the Lord.

Moving in the Spirit and not in the flesh makes for a very different, interesting and challenging lifestyle. Having experienced it I just want to live more and more in this way.

Prayer: Lord, teach me to move in your Spirit.

4th Guided

You will hear a voice behind you to guide you, saying, "This is the right path; follow it."
Isaiah 30.21

Finding myself in the right place at the right time is one of the fruits of walking in the Spirit. It makes each day a journey of discovery as I ask the Lord what he is going to do today.

From my end, it involves openness to his leadings and promptings as he brings people to me whom he wants to minister to in different ways.

Prayer: Lord, guide me into your ministry.

5th Ambassadors

You are ambassadors for Christ
2 Corinthians 5.20

My role as a believer in this world is to be an ambassador for Christ. I am his representative living in his embassy in a foreign land. I am a citizen of heaven and a living representative of the Kingdom of God.

This means that even in my most casual of dealings in this world I am here as a representative of Jesus Christ.

Prayer: Lord Jesus, make me a good ambassador for you.

6th The Manifestation of Christ

You do not realise this about yourselves that Jesus Christ is in you.
2 Corinthians 13.5

What I am measuring my life by is not how much money I have or the size of my house or my position in this world.

What is most important to me is how much of Christ is in me and how much of him is in what I do.

I am here in this world to manifest Christ, that is my purpose. Each day I am asking the Lord to increase his presence in me so that I may manifest him more fully in this world.

Prayer: Jesus, manifest your life in me.

7th Called to Know

Know me, from the least to the greatest.
Hebrews 8.11

At the heart of the new covenant is God's promise that it will be the birthright of his people that they will know him.

There will be no barriers of class or race or age because through new birth all God's people will come to know him.

God wants me to know him and it is my birthright through the new covenant that I can and should know Him.

Prayer: Lord, may I know you more and more.

8th Bricks Without Straw

Straw to make bricks.
Exodus 5.7

Many years ago, the Israelites were forced by their taskmasters to make mud and straw bricks without a supply of straw. The problem was that without the straw it was impossible to make real bricks that would last.

Without the living Christ within it is impossible to make Christians. You can create something that looks like the real thing but when the heat is on it will fall apart like bricks without straw.

Just as there was no substitute for straw there is no substitute for Jesus Christ in my heart. Without him, my life would fall apart.

Prayer: Lord Jesus, increase your presence in my heart.

9th Not Conformed

Be not Conformed.
Romans 12.2

To fit in with the world and to receive its approval and praise the church is continually being pressed into compromising itself.

What is true for the church is true for the individual Christian and therefore for me. The pressure to put the approval and acceptance of others over and above the approval of God has never been greater.

One compromise leads to another and so the descent on the slippery slope of worldliness gathers speed.

Prayer: Lord, I want to be conformed to your will not the way of the world.

10th Fitting In

Like all the others.
1 Samuel 8.5

Following Christ means that I can't always fit in or be like everybody else. I have a different master and it is his voice and his way that I am following not the ways of this world.

It is a strong temptation to want to fit in and be accepted or approved by the world. But I am being called by the Lord to testify against the world and its ways, especially when it is aligned with the enemy who is always trying to corrupt everybody and everything.

Prayer: Lord, help me to testify against the world and its corruption.

11th Rejected and Replaced

I am really the one they have rejected.
1 Samuel 8.7

When I am rejected by people it hurts. The prophet Samuel was deeply hurt when the people rejected his prophetic leadership in favour of the earthly and worldly rule.

They wanted to be like everybody else and they were not prepared to live under the direct government of God.

They wanted someone to tell them what to do and they were prepared to hand over the responsibility for their lives to an earthly Lord rather than to live under the direct rule of God.

This meant that the prophetic voice and the prophet were side-lined. The Lord explained that it was not Samuel who was being rejected but him.

I have to keep remembering this when I am being rejected for Christ.

Prayer: Lord, help me to remember who is being rejected.

12th Rejection Hurts

Blessed are ye, when men shall revile you, and persecute you, and shall say all manner of evil against you falsely, for my sake.
Matthew 5.11

It doesn't feel very blessed to be rejected by people, especially if you have been looking to them for approval and validation.

Being pulled down and even betrayed is tough but I know that my master has been there before me. He is not unable to sympathise with my situation.

Thankfully, I no longer need to fester over the pain and hurt of rejection as I can hand it over and move on.

Prayer: Jesus, thank you for taking the pain of my rejection and setting me free to love.

13th Defilement

The defilements of the world
2 Peter 2.20

A satanic strategy for the opposition to God's work in my life has been executed through defilement and corruption.

In my early years, the evil one hijacked my soul as I embraced the values, attitudes, habits, beliefs and rhythms of the world.

The biggest struggle in my new life in Christ has been to leave behind those worldly habits that so successfully hooked me up with the devil.

Prayer: Lord, cleanse me from the defilement and corruption of evil.

14th Having Escaped

Forsaking the right way, they have gone astray.
2 Peter 2.15

Having escaped the corruption of the world, I have been continually tripped up by the corruption of the church.

As I have escaped the fires of corruption in the world, I have run into a building for safety only to find that it is itself on fire.

In Church systems as with the world, the endorsement and promotion of corruption and moral compromise abounds and it is difficult not to get drawn onto its ground.

However reasonable the arguments sound and however personable the actors are, I have to remind myself that there can be no return to the cities of the plains.

Prayer: Lord, keep me away from all corrupting influences in the church.

15th Fading Glory

Fading though it was.
2 Corinthians 3.7

When I was young this world seemed to offer so much and it seemed as if this was the only reality.

As I am getting older the glory of this world has been fading as I realise that my life in this world is so fleeting.

This world with all its excitement and glitter is an all-consuming place but it does not last and its glory always fades.

I am an eternal being and I am made for eternity. My glory will be found in heaven, not on earth.

My life in this world may be fading but I am okay with it because each day I am coming closer to my real life which is awaiting me in heaven.

Prayer: Lord, thank you that glory awaits in heaven.

16th Moving in the Spirit

We live by the Spirit.
Galatian 5.25

Living and moving in the Spirit is a wonderful way to live. It is an amazing thing to know the Spirit urging me and directing my every move so that I am just where he wants me to be.

Not only am I in the right place at the right time but I am there with the message or the deed that is needed at that moment.

Having my life governed, timed and overseen by the Holy Spirit is an amazing experience as I find myself in situations which have been prearranged by him.

Moving in the Spirit and not in the flesh makes for a very different, interesting and challenging lifestyle.

Prayer: Lord, keep me moving in your Spirit.

17th We Have Fellowship

We have fellowship with one another.
1 John 1.7

Fellowship is far more than a cup of coffee and a chat after church. It is not about us in the first instance because the fellowship is first and foremost with Jesus Christ.

Fellowship in Christ means that through it Christ is being ministered to one another.

True fellowship takes place when Christ is being ministered to me through his life that is flowing in and through my brothers and sisters in Christ.

When that divine exchange is taking place then fellowship is happening. The measure of fellowship is not found in the number of people who are gathering but in how much of Christ is coming through.

The true test of fellowship is how much of Christ is being ministered to your spiritual life through me and how much of Christ is being ministered to my spiritual life through you.

Prayer: Lord Jesus, manifest your life through my fellowship.

18ᵗʰ The Desires

You will not gratify the desires of the flesh.
Galatians 5.16

God does not remove us from this world and neither does he take away the desires of our flesh that come from our original parents.

The desires of the flesh are multifaceted and they run deep as a result of our inheritance in Adam.

No matter how far I advance in my life in the Spirit I can never entirely escape the demands of my flesh.

God has not removed the desires but he does stop me from gratifying them by the power of his Holy Spirit who lives in me and is at work within me.

He gives me his thoughts and the power of choice so that I don't have to act on the demands of the flesh anymore.

Prayer: Lord, May I walk by your Spirit.

19ᵗʰ Intoxicating

Set your minds on things above.
Colossians 3.2

The world is very intoxicating and all-consuming. It is continually grabbing and demanding my total attention and devotion.

The material culture of this world is wanting to take over and become my only reality. It is therefore more important than ever that I am highly intentional about setting my mind on things above not on things on earth.

Prayer: Lord, keep my focus on heavenly reality.

20th From First to Last

A righteousness that is by faith from first to last.
Romans 1.17

The Apostle Paul talked about the scandal of the gospel and I know why. Righteousness with God comes through faith and not through my good behaviour.

I am declared righteous not because of anything in me but because of Christ. All I bring to the table is my faith in Jesus and the righteousness that he has given to me.

From the day I first believed until my last day on earth my righteousness is not and will never be something that I have made myself good enough to receive. It has come to me as a gift through my faith in Jesus.

Prayer: Lord Jesus thank you for the gift of your righteousness.

21st Fill Me

That you may be filled with all the fullness of God.
Ephesians 3.19

Fill me with your fullness Oh Christ.

Fill me with your life, your love and your Holy Spirit, as never before.

More of you Lord. Much more of you.

Increase your presence and your Spirit's anointing in my life.

More of you Lord Jesus, more of your fullness.

Prayer: Lord, fill me with your fullness.

22nd Who Stopped You?

You were running a good race who cut in on you and stopped you?
Galatian 5.7

I can identify the exact point early in my new life as a Christian where my faith was derailed. I was going with God in a most exciting and wholehearted way as my earnest faith paid off in my experience of a significant measure of the fullness of Christ.

Sadly, I was cut in on and stopped from pursuing this fullness of life in the Spirit as other more knowledgeable believers persuaded me to trade in my life of fullness for a more respectable form of faith that relied on human wisdom and power.

This resulted in many years of wandering in the wilderness until I found myself reaching out again in faith for the fullness that I had lost all those years before.

Prayer Lord Jesus, continue to restore your fullness in me.

23rd Not for Self

Those who live should no longer live for themselves but for him.
2 Corinthians 5.15

This is the big shift that has come to me since turning to Christ. My centre of gravity shifted and it continues to move away from myself to Christ so that I am increasingly no longer living for myself but him.

This is so much more than just turning up to church on Sunday morning plus a few good works in the community offered on my terms when I feel like it or want to make a good impression and feel good about myself.

This is the constant dethronement of self and self-interest that takes place as I live my life for Christ.

He died for me and now I die daily for him as I give up my life to make room for his. As I die to myself and my self-will so he lives in me and through me.

Prayer: Lord Jesus, I live for you not for myself.

24th Apparent Failure

He saved others let him save himself.
Luke 23.35

To the world, the cross is a symbol and a sign of failure. Everything about it screams failure and loss.

The cross looked like a total failure but in it was the greatest Victory that this world has ever seen, it just didn't look like it at the time.

Living in the light of the cross involves facing up to apparent failure in our lives as things don't look that good from a worldly perspective. We live in a world that demands obvious success usually in terms of achievement marked by popularity and money.

When we don't deliver on these terms we can be perceived as failures in the eyes of the world and yet this is often the way of the cross.

Prayer: Lord, may I embrace the failure of the cross as well as its victory.

25th Opposition

Our Struggle.
Ephesians 6.12

As soon as I press into the Lord for more, I hit up against opposition, particularly from my flesh.

My flesh is that fifth column within me that wants to assert itself and gets worried when it senses that it might have to move over to make more room for the Holy Spirit.

The enemy of my soul is also quick to counter any attempt by me to surrender more of my life to the Lord as I seek to have more of his Holy Spirit ruling and reigning within.

It can feel like two steps forward and one step back or sometimes one step forward and two steps back as the enemy redoubles his efforts to keep me where he wants me.

Prayer: Lord, overcome the opposition of my flesh to your Holy Spirit within.

26th Heart Knowledge

No one can say, "Jesus is Lord," except by the Holy Spirit.
1 Corinthians 12.3

I suppose that I could have said 'Jesus is Lord' before I came to him but I would not have meant it or believed it in its fullest sense.

I use to believe in Jesus as a good person who existed and had a significant ongoing impact on the lives of many.

However, I did not believe that he was Lord in the sense that he is over everything and in charge of this world and its future.

It was only through the work of the Holy Spirit in me that I came to know in my heart that Jesus Christ is Lord of everything including me.

Prayer: Holy Spirit, thank you for revealing the Lordship of Christ to me.

27th Human Viewpoints

We regard no one from a human point of view.
2 Corinthians 5.16

In my daily encounters with people, I am seeking God's heart for them. From my position in Christ, I am not just engaging with people on an earthly, natural and material level.

I am keeping one ear open to the Lord as I listen to the person who is talking or just standing there in front of me.

I set aside my preconceived ideas about them which are usually based on superficialities such as appearance or speech.

I find myself praying to be open to the Lord and asking him if there is anything he wants me to do or say.

Prayer: Lord, help me to see what you see and hear what you hear.

28th The Meditation of My Heart

The meditation of my heart.
Psalm 19.14

I pray every day that the Lord will direct my thinking so that it is on a higher plane than merely human thinking.

I am seeking the mind of Christ so that my thinking will be divorced from self-pity and selfish or dishonest motives.

I pray that throughout the day God will raise the meditations of my heart and mind so that I am in tune with his intentions and plans.

Prayer: Lord, may the meditations of my heart and mind be directed by you.

29th Saved

The son...in whom we have redemption.
Colossians 1.14

I am more conscious than ever before of my need for salvation. I need to be saved from my sin and myself.

I am my own worst enemy, a saboteur of God's good purpose in my life. I am sensing my desperate need for God and his mercy in my life.

I am more aware than ever of the hopelessness of my situation without God who has stepped in to save me and rescue me from my sinful self.

I need Jesus and his work of redemption, for, without it, I am without God and hope in the world.

Prayer: Holy Spirit thank you for making me aware of my desperate need for Jesus.

30th Hunger

Blessed, are those who hunger.
Matthew 5.6

I am experiencing an intense hunger in my heart for God. This experience of spiritual emptiness is very uncomfortable and I am looking for ways to fill this gaping hole in my heart.

I am bringing my neediness before the Lord and seeking to be filled with his Spirit and his life. Only God can provide the spiritual sustenance that I am hungry for. Only he will satisfy this intense hunger and need that I am feeling.

Prayer: Lord, fill my hungry heart.

October

1st Being Unimportant

I must decrease
John 3.30

The importance of being unimportant and the willingness to be so is at the heart of the spiritual journey.

As I go on with God and my knowledge of him increases, I am made more and more aware of my unimportance and my insignificance.

What is happening is that God is at work in me to get me right-sized and to draw me away from an over-inflated ego and an exaggerated sense of my own importance.

Prayer: Lord, may you continue to increase and may I continue to decrease.

2nd Out of My Mind

Peace, I leave with you; my peace I give to you.
John 14.27

I can understand why the phrase getting out of your mind has become common parlance. Many are the thoughts that besiege our minds each day and it is all too easy to be overwhelmed by them.

This is especially true when I sit down in silence to be still and quiet before the Lord. At such times my mind seems to go into overdrive in a desperate attempt to stay in control of everything.

I am not my mind and the way out of my overly busy mind is not through outside stimuli but through the discipline of interior silence and the peace that comes through communion with God.

Prayer: Lord, still my overly busy mind.

3rd Close the Door

When you pray, go into your room, close the door and pray.
Matthew 6.6

The act of closing the door is specifically mentioned by Jesus in his teaching about prayer. There is of course the practical and physical act of shutting the door of your room so that you remain undisturbed but I see a deeper meaning here.

When I come to pray and sit quietly in the presence of God many thoughts, ideas and images knock at the door of my mind as they seek to take my attention off the Lord.

In my prayers, I have been learning to close the door of my mind to the many unwanted mental visitors who seem to arrive at the very moment that I am seeking communion and fellowship with God.

Prayer: Lord, help me to close the door to the mental distractions in prayer.

4th Holding On

They left everything.
Matthew 4.20

If I hold onto the edge of the swimming pool, I won't drown but I will not be able to swim. The things, people and ideas that I hold onto for my security are often what is preventing me from moving forward and swimming well in the pool of life.

Like the poolside, old habits of thought and action have the feeling of security and safety but unless I let go of them, I will never learn to swim in the river of God's Spirit.

Prayer: Lord, release my grip on the unhelpful things that I am holding onto.

5th Letting Go

So, we must let go.
Hebrews 12.1

The continual process of letting go is at the heart of my journey with God. These two words are crucial to my life lived in communion with the Lord.

It sounds easy to let go but in practice, I find that my attachments are very strong and my sense of security is tightly bound up with the things that I am holding onto.

Prayer: Lord, help me to let go.

6th The Hearts Dialogue

Out of your heart shall flow rivers of living water.
John 7.38

The internal dialogue of my heart with God is a wonderful gift. The constant flow of communication between my heart and the heart of God is an amazing thing.

Much of this communion is in my expression of spontaneous praise, worship and adoration. It wells up from within me like the spring of living water that our Lord spoke about.

Prayer: Lord, thank you for flowing through my heart.

7th Total Dependence

My soul thirsts for thee.
Psalm 63.1

My inner dialogue with the Lord consists of copious prayers of dependence on Him. The monologue from my spirit consists of bursts of spontaneous prayers with phrases like 'Lord, I need you, I love you, Lord you are very beautiful, I praise you, thank you, Lord, thank you, Jesus, bless you, I love you Holy Spirit, Lord, help me.'

These prayers explode from within me and I am aware that it is not me who is making them happen.

They come from my inner man of the spirit and are not the product of my thinking or my mind. My mind tries to veto them in its quest for supremacy and control.

Prayer: Lord, I say yes to you and your prayers within me.

8th More than These

Do you love me more than these?
John 21.15

My renunciation of this world is an act of love for my Lord Jesus. This is not a sentimental or emotional love but a love that is expressed in concrete and tough decisions to go with him.

I love Jesus more than the opinions of others and more than the things of this world that so many people are chasing after.

My program for happiness is no longer centred on me and my selfish desires. My love for Jesus is overriding my love for myself.

This is the evidence of the Spirit's work within me.

Prayer: Jesus, I want to love you more.

9th Dogma

You teach rules made up by humans.
Matthew 15.9

Dogma dogs me every step forward in faith. I have been schooled in particular concepts of God that form an impregnable fortress of belief.

Should this dogma be challenged by some new truth the guard dog starts to growl and shows his teeth.

The more this new truth is revealed the more angry and nasty the dog becomes. Once the dogma is let off the lead it makes straight for the new truth, sinking its jaws and teeth into it as it tries desperately to destroy it.

When my dogma becomes blind prejudice then I need to beware that I may well be shutting out the very truth that will set me free for the next leg of my journey in faith.

Prayer: Lord, release me from religious prejudice and dogma.

10th No One is Righteous

No one is righteous not one.
Romans 3.10

It is tremendously liberating to know that my acceptance by God is not dependent on my performance.

My self-generated righteousness is of no value before the Lord because he is interested in truth in my innermost being.

He holds up the mirror of truth to my life so that I see myself as I am, not how I would like to portray or see myself.

Many are religious but no one is righteous which is why I need to be clothed with the righteousness of Jesus.

Prayer: Lord, thank you that I can come to you just as I am.

11th Transcendent Union

Be still and know.
Psalm 46.10

In silent and contemplative prayer, I experience what I would describe as times of transcendent union with God.

I used to think that I had just fallen asleep but that is not what is happening in such times. I sense that I am under the anaesthetic of God's presence and that he is performing soul surgery on me.

When I surface from these times, I have a deep sense of peace and relaxation. I believe that what is taking place is a transcendent divine union of my Spirit with the Spirit of the Lord.

There is no formula for this and no method other than sitting down with the intention of spending time in the presence of God.

Prayer: Lord, increase my awareness of our union.

12th Spiritual Possessiveness

Lord, it is good for us to be here…I'll make three shelters.
Matthew 17.4

When I have a positive spiritual experience like the sense of God's presence in me or with me then I want to hold onto it.

I want to keep hold of it and treasure it forever, but it can't be done. God is continually on the move and life is constantly changing so the only thing I can do is to let go of my memory of the experience and be open to the next encounter with God as he chooses to manifest himself.

As with possessions and material belongings, trying to hold on to spiritual experiences as if they belonged to me, just doesn't work.

They melt in my hands like ice cream on a hot sunny day.

Prayer: Lord, help me to be open to new experiences of you.

13th Healing Presence

The sun of righteousness shall arise with healing in his wings.
Malachi 4.2

In times of quiet contemplative prayer, God is present to heal me as he comes with healing in his wings.

I know this because as I live out my life in his presence there is evidence of a divine therapy having taken place.

This is not because I am trying to change as the transformation is coming from his healing presence within me.

These are not obvious or dramatic things but small changes that make a big difference to me and those around me.

Prayer: Lord, I open myself to your healing presence.

14th Deep Change

Be transformed.
Romans 12.2

Unless there is a deep work through the action of the Holy Spirit within me then nothing is going to change.

I can make superficial changes and resolve to be different but unless there is a deeper work in my inner man of the Spirit then there will be little change in the long run.

The deep and abiding changes in my life have come through the action of the Spirit of God at depth.

It is in times of transcendent union with God that the deeper work takes place. All I can do is put myself in the right place to receive and then accept whatever it is that God wants to give and to do.

Prayer: Lord, help me to surrender to your actions within me.

15th Experiencing God

That I might know him.
Philippians 3.10

I experience God who is in me and around me. He is not the far-off God. His nearness is a reality in my experience of life in this world.

God is the central pillar of my life as I walk moment by moment in his presence and his will. I regard myself as privileged as I know many people don't have this experience or perhaps, they don't believe it is possible.

God is invisible and supernatural which means that it is difficult for people to accept his real presence especially if they want to put God in a test tube and analyse him.

Ever since I first experienced God, I have wanted to share this experience with others so that they too might come to know him in their experience.

More than ever, I want people to experience God for themselves.

Prayer: Lord, help me to share my experience of you.

16th Filthy Rags

All our righteous deeds are filthy rags.
Isaiah 64.6

I am still heavily scripted in the idea that somehow, I have got to make myself good. I am deeply rooted in the notion that I need to achieve a religious and moral performance that will make me acceptable to God.

I have to keep reminding myself that when I am feeling exercised to justify myself through my self-righteous deeds, they are no better than filthy rags in comparison with God's work for my justification.

Prayer: Lord, help me to rely fully on the righteousness of Jesus Christ.

17th Self-Improvement

By Grace.
Ephesians 2.8

Self-improvement that is independent of the power and presence of God does not work for me.

I cannot be the person that God intends me to be through my efforts and strategies for growth.

It is only his program and not mine that will do the job in the long run. He is the trainer and the guide. He is the teacher and it is my intention to sit willingly under his instruction for the rest of my life.

Prayer: Lord, continue to teach me and train me.

18th Know Him

Know him.
Philippians 3.10

What I have realised over time is that many dear and sincere people even in our churches just don't know him.

At various times and places amongst good and faithful people I find myself saying, 'they don't know him.'

These are often people who are working for God and to the best of their knowledge they believe they are serving him faithfully, but there is no personal knowledge or experience of his presence at depth.

This spurs me on to know him and to love him even more so that I may be a signpost and a carrier of his real presence to those who don't know him or have never experienced his love.

Prayer: Lord, may my life carry your loving presence.

19th His Healing Presence

I am the Lord that healeth thee.
Exodus 15.26

Following times spent in the presence of the Lord in silent prayer things happen and those things are not always comfortable or easy.

God's presence is a healing presence and one of the by-products of my times of contemplative prayer is that there is a deep inner work of healing taking place in my heart.

There are times when the Lord seems to be particularly interested in dealing with something in me that I wasn't even aware of.

He removes the dressings that have been placed over my wounds and as he exposes them to his light so the healing takes place.

As with any wound that is healing there is discomfort and there is a dis-ease. It can be very uncomfortable and even painful as God peels back and removes layers of necrotic material so that he can apply his healing oil.

Prayer: Lord, continue your healing work in my heart.

20th Silence in Heaven

There was silence in heaven for about half an hour.
Revelation 8.1

We live in a world of noise and distraction. In such an environment silence can seem strange and even awkward.

We rush to fill the gaps in conversations fearing that we might all be left with an uncomfortable and embarrassing pause.

Being silent with God has been an important part of my journey of faith and as I get older, I value it increasingly.

It is in times of planned silence that I align my spirit with my true north who is the Lord of my life. This silent realignment locks me into his love for me and my love for him as I rest in the silence of his presence.

Prayer: Lord, commune with me in the silence of my heart.

21st Pressure

The Holy Spirit testifies to me that difficulties await me.
Acts 20.23

A life lived in fellowship with the Lord is not an easy life. In many ways, it is the hardest of all life's roads.

Inwardly there may be found deep inner peace but outwardly there is often pressure, distressing circumstances, trials and afflictions.

What helps me is knowing that these troubles are all part and parcel of life on the road to the heavenly city.

The obstacles and difficulties that I encounter on this road less travelled are all part of my personal journey into a life of willing dependence on the Lord.

Prayer: Lord I gladly accept the pressures and difficulties that come on this earthly pilgrimage.

22nd Trouble

In me, you may have peace. In the world, you will have trouble.
John 16.33

This is the great paradox in my life with God. On the one hand, I have to deal with life and all its tribulations but on the other hand, I can know God's peace in the most troubled of situations. My natural inclination is to want to avoid trouble and difficulties but that is not God's way.

This life of faith takes me on a higher and more difficult pathway that involves pain, suffering, struggle, difficulties and deprivation of different kinds. But in the middle of these very troubles is the place of peace, joy and love that comes at such times from the Lord of Hosts.

Prayer: Lord, may I find your peace, amongst the troubles of this world.

23rd Self-Defence

Vengeance is mine, I will repay.
Romans 12.19

We are all born with innate self-defence mechanisms so that when we feel threatened, we move quickly to defend ourselves.

My natural defence mechanisms have their place but I have to make sure that they don't move me into making pre-emptive strikes or retributive moves against people who have acted aggressively towards me.

Under the motivation of hidden anger, I can take matters into my own hands by fighting back and seeking to inflict punishment on those who have hurt me.

I am learning to let go and to give room for the Lord to defend me by bringing his judgment and justice to the situation in his own time.

Prayer: Lord, I trust you to defend me.

24th Bound Over

Let the peace of Christ rule in your hearts.
Colossians 3.15

In Christ, I have been bound over to keep the peace. Living in the new man I am constantly seeking to dwell in the peace of the Lord.

At the same time as I seek God's rest, the world is trying to call me out from that place of peace and onto its territory of anxiety, turmoil and conflict.

I have been bound over to keep the peace and through meditation and prayer, I am seeking to live my life on the basis of rest and peace.

Prayer: Lord, bind me over to keep your peace in my heart.

25th By Searching

Can we by searching find God?
Job 11.7

God is so much greater than anything or anyone that I can even think of or imagine. All the metaphors and anthropomorphic ideas that he has given to us about himself do not do justice to his majesty and his greatness.

It is therefore not surprising that as a human being I cannot by my searching or reasoning find God.

God has to reveal himself for me to connect with him. It is he that initiates, and it is I who need to respond.

Prayer: Lord, continue to reveal yourself in me and to me.

26th His Teaching

The Spirit of revelation.
Ephesians 1.17

The teaching that is impacting me most is that which is coming directly from Jesus. He is making me aware of particular scriptures and then he is teaching them to me so that I can appreciate their meaning and power.

Some of these scriptures are well-known to me but others are from outside the realm of my conscious memory or knowledge.

This is a supernatural thing as I set aside my so-called knowledge and open myself to the teacher, who is Jesus.

Prayer: Lord, keep me listening for your teaching.

27th The Outer Appearance

An impressive young man.
1 Samuel 9.2

I find it helpful to reflect on the fact that behind the hard exterior of some great man there is often a frightened little boy.

The outer shell is tough and seemingly impenetrable to emotion but underneath there is a heart that is hungry and desperately in need of the liquid love of God.

The great danger is that with constant neglect the heart becomes increasingly hardened and almost incapable of receiving the love that it so desperately needs.

Prayer: Lord, give me a heart that is ever open to you.

28th Acting Independently

Have you eaten from the tree which I commanded you not to eat?
Genesis 3.11

The great mistake of our ancestors which I constantly repeat is to act independently of God. The challenge for me in this life is to allow the influence of the Holy Spirit to counter the spirit of independence that is so deeply rooted within me.

In a world that seeks independence at every level, I am practising an increasingly radical level of dependence on the Lord as his Spirit steers me and leads me into his ways.

Prayer: Lord, I renounce independence and seek to depend solely on you.

29th Getting Centred

If anyone would come after me let him deny himself.
Matthew 16.24

As a son of Adam, I am inherently self-centred and not God-centred. My 'go-to' reference point in my decisions and actions is myself. My best thinking, what I want, and what I feel are thereby given the reigns of my life.

The key to my ongoing life with God is the continual dethronement of this self-life and the enthronement of the Holy Spirit as I submit my thinking, feeling, and doing to him.

This decentring of self is aided as I step aside from active life through the practice of silent prayer where I make room for the Lord to re-centre me.

This keeps me on his path rather than going off on some self-directed excursion in self-will.

Prayer: Lord, keep my life centred in you.

30th Waiting Patiently

I waited patiently for the Lord.
Psalm 40.1

In my natural self, I find it difficult to wait. The idea of waiting on God does not come easily to me.

I want to jump in to try to fix things or to move them along using my impatient chasing and pushing to make something happen.

These actions are usually unfruitful and often counter-productive as they tend to cause more problems than they solve.

I want to pre-empt God and get tomorrow's answers today, but in my haste, I can run ahead of him and go way off track.

Prayer: Lord, help me to wait for you.

31st Learning Christ

Learn Christ.
Ephesians 4.20

Life, with all its attendant ups and downs, affords me the opportunity to learn Christ. It is in the uncertainty and sometimes confusion of everyday life that I get the opportunity to learn and then walk in his ways.

I often want to get to the end of the learning process when it has only just begun. I want to bypass the difficulties and the joys of each day in my quest to fast forward my life by scrolling too quickly through the lessons of each season.

I am realising that God wants me to value and enjoy the process of learning Christ in my circumstances however challenging they may seem to be.

Prayer: Lord, help me to appreciate my learning of Christ in every circumstance of life.

November

1st Soul Force

> *I will say to my soul.*
> *Luke 12.19*

The unholy trinity of my independent self-life operates through the force of my will, my feelings, and my thinking.

Ungoverned, my self-life expressed through soul force exerts pressure on me to conform to its desires and demands for attention.

My soul can make me feel uncomfortable and ill at ease. It can fill my mind with obsessive thoughts and it can attach my will to any passing attraction of the body, mind or emotions.

I am not unaware of its pressures and when it is strong within, the best antidote is for me to take time out with God.

It is here, in the presence of the Lord that my soul force is uncovered, disarmed and disempowered by the light of God's Spirit.

Prayer: Lord, keep me living from the power of your Spirit within.

2nd Soul Life

> *Whoever would come after me must deny himself.*
> *Matthew 16.26*

Self-denial is at the heart of my walk as a believer. What it means is the denial of my soul's strength and power in favour of the Spirit's power that comes only from God.

I have to deny everything that comes from my self-centred soul life so that what I am, what I do, and what I have, come entirely from the Lord.

I can live by the power of my soul using my cleverness or I can deny that source and live instead by the power of the Holy Spirit who dwells within my spirit.

The self-denial that Jesus is talking about is the denial of my natural soul power as I allow myself to be led and empowered by the Holy Spirit.

Prayer: Lord, teach me to deny myself and to live by the Spirit.

3rd God's Thought

To die is gain.
Philippians 1.21

In times of quiet prayer, I am seeking the Lord. I am not looking for feelings or sensations but I am seeking the development of my relationship with him and his relationship with me.

As I abide in his presence, I am setting aside my best thinking, my will and my feelings. I am tuning into God's thoughts, God's will and God's way.

In letting go of my soul life and through handing it over to death, I am preparing my soul for the resurrection of his life in me.

As I die to my natural self-life it is his life that is being resurrected in me as my soul is raised with him and my life bears fruit for eternity.

Prayer: Lord, help me to die to self that I may live for you.

4th Everything You Have

You cannot be my disciple unless you give up everything you have.
Luke 14.33

It's easy to water down or try to explain away the teaching of Jesus so it's important not to let it lose its full impact.

The nature of being a disciple of Jesus involves being willing to give up everything you have including your life.

My experience of this is that I am giving up more and more of myself to him. I am handing over and surrendering my life in increasing measure to the Lord.

Prayer: Lord, all that I am I give to you.

5th All Rubbish

I have suffered the loss of all things and I count them rubbish.
Philippians 3.8

The apostle who wrote this and many who have come after him have finished their lives in prison having suffered the loss of all things for their testimony about Jesus.

His great learning and education as well as his inherited status and social position were all abandoned in his life of obedience to his master.

His honour and reward were not in this life or this world, as he rejected its values and suffered the loss of everything this world considers of value.

Faced with such a choice I wonder how I would do. I suspect that by the grace of God and the power of the Spirit within me, I too would count all things rubbish for the sake of Christ Jesus my Lord.

Prayer: Lord, help me to let go of this world and hold fast to Jesus Christ.

6th Relying on God

This happened that we might not rely on ourselves but on God, who raises the dead.
2 Corinthians 1.9

Self-reliance and self-sufficiency are signs that I still have a way to go on my journey with God. To strip me of my reliance on self-sufficient soul power the Lord takes me into situations where I am way outside my ability to cope.

I find myself in circumstances where I have to rely on God to get me through. In these times I know that I have reached the end of myself and that God wants me to rely fully and completely on him.

It is as I experience this death of self that I find God raising me from the dead and restoring my trust and hope in him.

Prayer: Lord, raise me through the death of self.

7th Indestructible

Do not fear those who kill the body but cannot kill the soul.
Matthew 10.28

Jesus's death along with his subsequent resurrection confirms for me the indestructibility of my soul through the eternal life of God within.

My human soul has been vivified by the indwelling presence of the Holy Spirit and is therefore indestructible.

God will not destroy his own life, and it is that life that is in me. My body may be smashed to pieces or even incinerated but by the Holy Spirits' birth and life within me, my revived soul and spirit will never die.

Prayer: Lord, thank you for the gift of eternal life.

8th Death before Life

Unless a seed falls to the ground and dies it cannot bear fruit.
John 12.24

I believe in death before life. It sounds quite shocking but what I mean by this is what the early disciples of Jesus called death to self.

My old natural self is so corrupted that it cannot be raised no matter how much effort and determination I throw at it.

There is no way that my flesh can develop spiritually. The only way forward is for my old nature to die like a seed that falls to the ground before it is regenerated and can produce fresh fruit.

This is so much more radical than merely a reformation of the old self-life. It is a completely new life following the death of the old one.

Prayer: Lord, help me to die to my old self and to live from the new.

9th My Soul Gasps

When shall I come and appear before God?
Psalm 42.2

I get world-weary as I have to deal with the realities of life. As I do so I find myself longing to get into the presence of the Lord.

I experience longing and a sense of desperation like a diver needing oxygen. I find myself gasping for the breath of God to breathe his life into me.

I take every opportunity to steal away to be with the Lord and it is always a relief. As I take time out with him, I find his life refreshing me and renewing my strength.

Prayer: Lord, my soul gasps for you, for the living God.

10th Building on the Rock

A wise man who built his house on the rock.
Matthew 7.24.

When I am focussing my attention on my flesh and paying too much attention to my old self I am building on sand. No amount of energy or work can ever change my flesh and the more attention I give it the more it will grow in its power over me.

Instead, I am focussing my attention on my new life in the Spirit built on the foundation of the cross as I seek the will of God through the direction of the Holy Spirit.

When I realise that I am being pulled off course by my flesh I return my attention to the Lord and reaffirm my intention to be his. This all happens in a nano-second and multiple times a day as it is more and more of an automatic response in my walk with the Lord.

This is what is meant by building on the rock as my life is being constructed under the guidance of the master builder on the foundations laid by his son.

Prayer: Lord, help me to build only on you and not my flesh.

11th Co-Crucifixion

I have been crucified with Christ.
Galatians 2.20.

I have not been physically crucified with Christ but spiritually I have been crucified as my self-life and my flesh have been denied and mortified.

As I have followed the master, I have been betrayed, bullied, slandered, manipulated, controlled, used, mocked, ridiculed, scoffed at, flattered, conned, lied to, deceived, plotted against, stabbed in the back, blamed, shamed, intimidated, and threatened.

These crosses have come to me as I have sought to walk by the Spirit in the situations that the Lord has placed me in.

The temptation has always been to run away from the cross and the consequent death to self. Thankfully by the grace of God, I have been able to resist and to stick with this co-crucifixion. I can now say that I have been crucified with Christ.

Prayer: Lord, thank you for the cross.

12th The Lamp of the Lord

The spirit of man is the lamp of the Lord.
Proverbs 20.27.

My spirit was dead like a candle lamp without a flame. It wasn't until my spirit was touched and set alight by the Spirit of the Lord that I became spiritually alive.

That flame can never be snuffed out but it can be hidden and covered so that it doesn't shine as brightly as it could.

As I spend time in the presence of the Lord, he increases his presence within me and my spirit is aglow.

Prayer: Lord, may I be aglow with you.

13th The Truth

You shall know the Truth.
John 8.32.

We are instructed to develop understanding but this injunction goes one step further. Jesus promises that I shall know the truth, but the knowing that he is talking about is different from just a superficial understanding.

I can have an intellectual grasp of the truth without knowing it in my life and experience. My experience of the truth depends on a deep knowing in my soul and spirit that is followed by continual growth in my understanding.

Increasingly, I not only understand the truth that the Lord is teaching me but I also know it and really 'get' it at depth. What was previously head knowledge has become real in my experience and life.

Prayer: Lord, may I know you more than I understand you.

14th Soul Music

I will say to my soul, soul.
Luke 12.19.

I have spent too much of my life living in my soul. Instead of tuning into the heavenly melodies of the Spirit of the Lord, I have been listening to the wrong music.

I have been living in my soul instead of living in my spirit and the result has been discord. Now I am learning to live from my spirit and not from my soul.

Instead of listening to the music of my soul, I am learning to tune into the melody of the Spirit.

Prayer: Lord, I choose to live by your Spirit and not by my soul.

15th Consider Him

Consider him who endured from sinners such hostility against himself.
Hebrews 12.3.

God uses opposition and rejection to purge me of my fleshy desire for the acceptance and approval of the world.

As I move forward in the will of God, I find myself up against opposition and rejection from those who are wanting a cross-less Christianity.

Jesus was popular and well-received and he attracted a considerable following until he started to teach that the cross would not only be his destiny but also that of all those who would truly follow after him.

Immediately he began to teach this he faced opposition, increasing rejection and ultimately death.

Prayer: Lord, help me to endure and grow through opposition and rejection.

16th The Witness

The Spirit himself bears witness with our spirit.
Romans 8.16.

God's life is in me by his Spirit and it is the life of his Spirit that is the witness to his presence within me.

Not only does the Spirit provide a witness within me to my sonship but to many other things as well.

He is the Spirit of truth and he witnesses to the truth of a matter. He is the one who brings his word to life so that it hits home to the inner man of my spirit.

The witness of the Spirit brings the word of the Lord to life in my experience and makes it all real.

Prayer: Lord, increase the witness of your Spirit in my spirit.

17th Sand and Rock

Foundations.
Matthew 7.25.

In the parable of the housebuilders, there are two possible foundations. One house is built on rock and the other is built on sand. The foundations are hidden and all that can be seen are the visible structures of the two buildings.

These buildings represent the two foundations for any life. One is built on Christ, the other is built on self. Every human life has these two possible foundations. One is Christ and the other is the human self.

Often well hidden, the self-life is founded in self-interest, self-preservation, self-justification, self-assertion, self-will and every other form of self-centred living.

Prayer: Lord Jesus, build your life in me and on you.

18th A Face Full of God

His face was like the face of an angel.
Acts 6.15.

I want to shine for God. I am seeking to be so full of the Holy Spirit of Jesus that my face glows.

I want eyes of blazing fire that transmit the life and the love of the Lord to all who I meet. I want to reflect the brightness of his glory into even the darkest and most hopeless corners of this world.

Prayer: Lord, may my face shine with your light.

19th Stumble and Fall

Many will stumble, fall and be broken.
Isaiah 8.15.

It is very embarrassing to trip up and fall when walking along a street full of people. It is all too easy to get distracted and fail to see the trip hazard that is in front of me. I need to take heed lest I stumble and fall.

Stumbling and falling are part and parcel of walking with the Lord in this world. I get tripped up by others as well as by the desires of my flesh that knock me off balance and take me down.

There is no room for complacency and no believer however advanced can afford to ignore the slippery terrain of this world.

Prayer: Lord, keep me from stumbling and falling.

20th Without Me

Without me, you can do nothing.
John 15.5.

In the power of my soul, I can do many things without God if I want to. I can exclude him and push him aside as I exercise my right to run my life my own way and do things as I see fit.

But if I want to do anything of eternal value that fulfils the purposes of God, then I need to cooperate with him and work in submission to his divine will.

Prayer: Lord, I confess that without you I can do nothing of eternal worth.

21st Waiting on the Lord

My soul waits in silence for God only.
Psalm 62.1.

I am not trying to initiate or do anything out from myself. I am resisting the urge and the pressure from my soul that wants to initiate and act out of independence from the Lord.

There is an inner conflict between my soul and the Spirit of the Lord who is restraining me and holding me back from acting out from myself.

As I submit to the Spirit my soul rebels with its endless list of things that it tells me I should be doing.

My soul brings forcefully before my consciousness all its desires and distractions to fill my mind with thoughts and schemes that render me unavailable to the Lord.

Prayer: Lord, may I wait on you alone.

22nd Soul Rest

Be Still.
Psalm 46.10.

The antidote to my restlessness is rest. Resting doesn't necessarily mean doing nothing or sitting with my feet up watching the television. True rest is more of an inherent predisposition and faculty that is given by God.

St Augustine said that our souls are restless till they find their rest in God. So, just how can we find this soul rest?

What I have learned is that my rest has its genesis in the times that I have set aside to be in the presence of the Lord. It is in the place of stillness before the Lord that I find true rest.

Learning to be rather than to do or to buzz around whilst flitting from one thing to the next is a fruit of time spent in the presence of the Lord.

There are no shortcuts to God's rest as it comes only from time spent in stillness with a growing awareness of God's presence and peace in knowing.

Prayer: Lord, help me to eschew my restlessness so that I may find my rest in you.

23rd Not One

No one is righteous, not one.
Romans 3.10.

None of us is better than anyone else. As God says: 'all have sinned and fall short of the glory of God.'

My righteousness is 'imputed' which means that it is conferred on me as a result of what Christ achieved on the cross and not as a result of anything that I have done.

This means that my position before God and his relationship with me are not dependent on my religious or moral performance.

Prayer: Lord, keep me right-sized and humble.

24th The Sanctuary

Until I went into the sanctuary of the Lord.
Psalm 73.17.

I need to regularly enter the sanctuary of the Lord through my times of meditation and prayer.

I enter with a head full of the world with its problems and injustices, that all seem so big and overwhelming.

But when I enter into the presence of the Lord, I get a new perspective which is quite different from the world around me.

What stressed me when I went in doesn't seem such a problem now. My tension seems to have gone and I have found peace of mind.

The world has a habit of taking over my mind as the urgent matter in front of me demands to be dealt with now, so there is no time for the Lord.

Hence my need to practice meditation as I go into the sanctuary of the Lord.

Prayer: Lord, help me to go regularly into your sanctuary.

25th When All Is Stripped Away

We brought nothing into this world, and it is certain we can carry nothing out.
1 Timothy 6.7.

Dying means leaving everything behind. The only thing we take with us is our soul and our spirit. The only thing we can keep is our relationship with God.

For our name to be known in heaven is far more important than having our name known on earth. But it's more than having our name known, it's about being known as a person by the Lord.

This happens over a lifetime if we want it. It is happening now all over the world as believers in Jesus focus their attention on his presence and his action in their lives.

When I die, I expect the transition to be seamless as I move out of God's veiled presence in this world and into the full glare of his glory.

Prayer: Lord, please help me to know you better now.

26th Silence

There was silence in heaven for half an hour.
Revelation 8.1.

I once heard, an old monk saying that I should keep in mind that God's first language is silence.

Coming from a tradition and a culture that is saturated with words and speech this was quite a challenge to me.

I am reminded of my Lord who said 'you think you will be heard because of your many words'.

Prayer for me is not just about speaking, it's about being, and that means being silent because silence is God's first language.

Prayer: Lord, may I speak your language of silence.

27th A Great Journey

This is the way walk in it.
Isaiah 30.21.

This journey into increasing divine union is a glorious one that I wouldn't trade for the world.

All those years I spent trying to fix myself in different ways have been replaced by an ever-expanding fellowship with God who is here and is within me.

The answer was here all the time and whilst my searching has in the past taken me way off course, I am now living the life that I was always meant to live.

Prayer: Lord, thank you for this wonderful journey into you and into life.

28th Enjoy Life

Enjoy Life.
Ecclesiastes 9.9.

Life is meant to be enjoyed not just endured. The only caveat to this in the Bible is that we are to find our enjoyment in legitimate and wholesome things rather than illegal and destructive activities.

I can get over-focussed on goal-oriented tasks to the point where I am failing to enjoy the journey and the ever-changing scenery of my life.

I have to remember to relax, take it easy, and enjoy my life as the Lord intended.

Prayer: Lord, help me to enjoy my life.

29th Not Slow

The Lord is not slow as some count slowness.
2 Peter 3.9.

My lack of patience manifests itself in the desire I have to push and force things to move forward according to my timescale.

These attempts to make something happen that emanate from my self-life rather than the life of the Spirit, are invariably doomed to failure or frustration of some kind.

God is not slow but I need to learn to be patient and to accept that the Lord is being patient with me and allowing the necessary changes to take place in me.

Prayer: Lord, thank you for your patience with me.

30th Simplicity of Life

Carry no purse, bag or sandals.
Luke 10.4.

Increasingly, I value simplicity in life. It seems to be much more conducive to life in the Spirit than a life packed full of this world and its interests.

Keeping my life simple is work in itself in a world that is increasingly complicated. All I can do is keep my desire and intention towards simplicity in the forefront of my mind as I journey through the complex maze of life.

In a world that is always calling out for more, I want less. I am living on the basis that less is more, and as I do so, I find I have more room for God.

Prayer: Lord, help me to live a simple life.

December

1st Spiritual Healing

You are set free from your infirmity.
Luke 13.12.

Jesus healed a woman who for eighteen years had suffered under a spirit of infirmity that had a serious physical effect on her body. She was not only in poor health but also bent over and unable to straighten up.

Once Jesus engages in spiritual healing and cleansing the woman is set free from her spiritual bondage and as a result, she can stand up straight.

The purpose of bringing ourselves before the Lord in times of quiet is to put ourselves in the position of consent so that he can do his deep and hidden work of healing and deliverance in our souls.

It is in this secret place of the Lord's abiding presence where deep spiritual healing and transformation take place long before it is manifested in our physical life.

Prayer: Lord, continue your work of spiritual healing in my life.

2nd Possessing Everything

Having nothing yet possessing everything.
2 Corinthians 6.10.

In a world that judges and evaluates you by what you possess it is reassuring to know that whilst I may be materially poor, I am spiritually rich.

Indeed, the whole thrust of my spiritual journey is one of a continuous letting go of the things that I hold onto, and that possess me, to take hold of the greater spiritual possessions that come through union with God.

The spiritual treasures that I now possess cannot be taken away from me as they are eternal and non-material.

Prayer: help me to let go of everything that is possessing me.

3rd God is Love

God is love.
1 John 4.16.

Perhaps the most important revelation about God in the Bible is that he is Love. Love is who God is and he has made me to live in the awareness and light of his love.

If I abide in God's presence then he lives in me and through me as I radiate and transmit his love.

This life of faith is all about love. God's love for me, in me and through me. I love because he first loved me and his love increases as I consent to his abiding and loving presence within me.

Prayer: Lord, help me to abide in your love.

4th Watch

Watch and pray.
Matthew 26.41.

The word used by Jesus when he instructs his disciples to watch and pray means to be attentive.

Watching in prayer means being attentive to God as I focus my attention on him and him only.

As the disciples discovered it's not always easy to do this as we can so quickly get distracted or even fall asleep.

Watching involves waiting and for that I need patience. In times of meditation and prayer, it's easy to quit too early or to give up because nothing seems to be happening.

I now know that even when it seems that nothing is going on there can be quite a lot happening as God honours my intention to be with him and sit quietly in his presence.

Prayer: Lord, help me to wait on you.

5th Beyond Thinking

My thoughts are not your thoughts.
Isaiah 55.8.

God is beyond my thinking, my feeling, or any kind of theological reflection that I might do. This does not mean that I can't think about him but what it does mean is that I can only come to know him beyond these things.

God is beyond my experience or my reflective ability because he is accessible only through faith. God comes to me as he wills and as he wants when I turn my face towards him in faith and love.

I cannot know him with my mind only with my love. God is beyond me and it is only through entering into what the mystical theologians call the cloud of unknowing that I can get to know him.

My experience has been that it is through unknowing what I think I know about God that I have come to know him in a dynamic and real way.

Prayer: Lord, help me to know you.

6th Pure Faith

Faith is the substance.
Hebrews 11.1.

Early on in my search for God, I had a pure and neat faith that was undiluted and unpolluted.

God honoured my pure faith by revealing himself to me in a very remarkable and tangible way.

I knew very little and had just a few fragments of Christian teaching but that was no obstacle to God as I had the one thing that mattered, and that was pure faith.

It was my simple faith that opened the door for the Lord and it is pure faith that continues to be the way into his presence.

Prayer: Lord, keep my faith pure and simple.

7th Non-Conceptual Prayer

I will pray with my spirit.
1 Corinthians 14.15.

The idea that we can pray not only with our minds but also with our spirits is an important one for me.

Having been schooled in western theology and spirituality I have tended to focus only on prayers that I could understand with my mind and I was suspicious of anything that I couldn't understand.

Non-conceptual prayer in the form of silent meditation has been an eye-opener for me. Learning to sit intentionally in the presence of God has opened me up to a new and wonderful life of prayer and communion with God.

Prayer: Lord, teach me to pray, even without words.

8th Being with Him

> *They had been with Jesus.*
> *Acts 4.13.*

As I spend time every day in the secret place with my Lord it is my earnest desire that something of him will rub off on me and be carried by me into the day.

It was noted that although they were not sophisticated by the standards of the day, the disciples of Jesus had something about them, and it was acknowledged that this was the result of their being with Jesus.

They not only carried the message verbally, but they were also the message, as the transforming presence of Christ was visible and identifiable in their lives.

Prayer: Lord, may your presence be manifest in my life.

9th It's Your Calling

> *To this, you were called.*
> *1 Peter 2.21.*

It took me a long time to figure out what God was calling me to in this life. Despite a clear initial call, there have been times when I have felt lost and wondered where my life is going and if I am on the right path.

It's only now as I look back that my pathway through life makes sense. I can now see that it all ties up and has been coming together in a most marvellous way. I could never have planned this path or made it happen on my own. My calling now makes sense in a way that it has never done before.

As I have followed my calling, I have been tempted to leave the path but I have always been prevented from making false moves at all the crucial points in my pilgrimage.

Prayer: Lord even if I don't understand my calling, I trust you with my life.

10th Open Doors

If anyone hears my voice and opens the door, I will come in.
Revelation 3.20.

I have been greatly helped by this picture in the Revelation of St John of opening the door of my soul to God's presence.

As many have pointed out the handle is on the inside. We have to consent as God will not force himself upon us.

These days the challenge for me is focused on keeping the door open to God by not giving my ego and false self-power over my spiritual life to eclipse God and thereby shut the door to his healing presence.

One way that I keep the door open is through the discipline of daily times of communion through the liturgy of silence in contemplative prayer.

I find that these daily times of silent prayer create space so that the Lord can come and fellowship with me.

Prayer: Lord, help me to keep the door open to you.

11th Personal Sin

Go and sin no more.
John 8.11.

Personal sin reinforces my false self. Upfront it seems attractive and can provide a temporary means of escape from my insecurity and my underground emotional pain.

My sin manifests in my desires for position, possession, power, pleasure, security, affection and esteem. Deeply rooted as habits, my sin has been hardwired into the core of my personality so that it is difficult to break free.

I find it helpful to keep in mind the fact that I don't want to build up my false self or give it any more fuel. Instead, I want to invest in behaviours that build up my true self where my centre of gravity is not me but God.

Prayer: Lord, help me to break free from all life-controlling habits.

12th God's Work

He who began a good work will bring it to completion.
Philippians 1.6.

Healing, wholeness and salvation are all God's work, not mine. Having begun his good work in me he will not stop until he has finished the job.

We are God's workmanship and he is the master craftsman. As I continue to consent to his presence and action in me his work continues apace and I can see the results in the gradual transformation of my life.

I am his workmanship from start to finish. I bear his hallmark and I am confident that he will bring his work in me to a wonderful conclusion.

Prayer: Lord, thank you that you will finish your work in and through me.

13th Prayer

When you pray.
Matthew 6.6.

What is prayer? Prayer is communication with God. I find it important to remember that the God I pray to is so much bigger and greater than me or my thinking. My mind cannot conceive how great and awesome God is.

So, when I pray and communicate with God, I am engaging with a power who is so much greater than me.

It is in silent prayer when I am still and quiet that I become most aware of God's presence and his peace that goes way beyond my understanding.

At such times there is communication and communion with my God. I am in contact with the God who created the universe. How marvellous is that?

Prayer: Lord, thank you for the gift of prayer.

14th Feeling God's Presence

If the presence does not go with us.
Exodus 33.15.

One of the most wonderful things in my life is the time that I spend in conscious contact with God. The awareness of his presence is so reassuring and comforting.

My awareness of God's abiding presence comes and goes because it is not in my control. It's not a technique or a faculty that I possess, rather it is a gift and a grace that I willingly receive with joy.

Knowing and feeling God in me and with me is something that I can cultivate or resist, and that is up to me.

Often, when I am sitting in silent prayer, I sense his nearness and his power, but he is the God of surprises and has a habit of showing up at the most unexpected times and in the most unlikely of places.

Prayer: Lord, thank you for your wonderful presence.

15th The Cares of this World

The worries of this life come in and choke the word.
Mark 4.19.

The world and its cares have the power to crush and drive out all thoughts of eternity and God.

We have been warned of this danger as the world works relentlessly to choke the spiritual life out of us.

Some days I struggle to rise above the domination of the urgent and pressing needs that are calling for my total attention.

It is only in prayer that I can truly find the detachment that I need and the peace that flows from it.

Prayer: Lord, keep me from being consumed by this world.

16th Impossible Situations

Without faith it is impossible.
Hebrews 11.6.

Faith involves us in situations that we may otherwise have avoided. At times we find ourselves having to learn to live with seemingly impossible circumstances.

The temptation is to want to run away or to find some form of a temporary quick fix. At such times my instinct is to want to escape to avoid the negative experience and the associated feelings of discomfort.

What I know from experience is that such times of extreme discomfort are often the times when I have grown the most in my faith and knowledge of God.

It is in the refiners-fire of difficulty that my character has been forged and beaten into shape.

Prayer: Lord, thank you for impossible situations.

17th Intellectual Arrogance

Humble Yourselves.
1 Peter 5.6.

The potential arrogance of the human intellect is immense. Our innate ability to overrate our intellectual prowess defies all logic.

It is easy to get caught up in the intellectual arrogance of an age that wants to pit its mind against God. But the reality is that compared to God's mind our intellect is on a par with that of the grasshopper.

The mind of God is universal but mine is finite. God is the mind behind all minds. He is the creator of all intelligent life.

I am just a created being and I am clear about the fact that I am not God.

Prayer: Lord, keep me humble and teachable.

18th Doing Nothing

Without me, you can do nothing.
John 15.5.

Jesus modelled and taught the importance of doing nothing in our strength and from our wisdom and power.

He was constantly referring back to his Father to check that he was doing and saying only what his Father wanted him to do and say.

It is all too easy to launch out into doing our own thing and speaking or acting independently of the Lord.

Without God, I can do nothing of lasting and eternal value. That's why I am seeking to move and stay in the centre of his will in all things, at all times, and in all places.

Prayer: Lord, keep me in the centre of your will in all things.

19th Resting in the Presence

You will find rest for your soul.
Matthew 11.29.

Coming from an activist background the idea of resting in God has taken me a long time to appreciate.

It is only as I have begun to intentionally give time to rest in God's presence that I have been blessed with a more consistent awareness of his peace.

I have also found that the interior silence and stillness in times of deep rest with God are reflected in my daily life.

Increasingly, I live from a place of inner stillness, rest and serenity rather than emotional turmoil and haste.

Prayer: Lord, increase my rest in you.

20th Lost and Found

He was lost.
Luke 15.24.

I was always under the impression that it was me who found God because I went looking for him.

It turns out that my awakening wasn't the result of my search, God was looking for me.

I was lost and I didn't have a map. I knew that there was a reality beyond this one but I just couldn't find my way to it.

In the end, God came out to find me and he brought me home rejoicing.

Prayer: Lord thank you for finding me.

21st Let it Go

A time to throw away.
Ecclesiastes 3.6.

One of the positive effects of my daily time of silent and contemplative prayer life has been in the area of my thought life.

In contemplative prayer, all sorts of distracting thoughts come into my mind as I sit down in silence and seek to centre myself in God.

In prayer, I have had to learn to let go of my thoughts and not obsessively hold onto them no matter how distracting and insistent they are.

This process of letting my thoughts go has seeped into my ordinary life as I have learned to throw away much of the junk that my mind can throw at me.

Important as these faculties are, my thinking and my mind are not my true self, and in daily life, it has been helpful to learn to let go of my unwanted thoughts.

Prayer: Lord, help me to let go of unwanted thoughts.

22nd True Freedom

The glorious liberty of the sons of God.
Romans 8.21.

There is wonderful and incomparable interior freedom in Christ that has been described as the glorious liberty of the sons of God. It's far greater than a mere experience.

It is much more akin to a transcendent sense of being above and outside of oneself and one's circumstances.

This glorious liberty comes as an internal awareness that I am in a spacious place with the Lord and no matter what is happening externally, I am free from its mental and emotional grip.

This self-transcendent freedom is akin to what the scripture describes as being raised up with wings like eagles.

It is true freedom.

Prayer: Lord, increase my internal freedom.

23rd Laughter

A joyful heart is good medicine.
Proverbs 17.22.

Humour and laughter are part of God's nature. His creation is full of humour and God is not above a good laugh.

You can see this in some of God's stories like Jonah when the plant that God has raised up to protect the prophet gets removed by a worm. You can almost hear God laughing at Jonah's remonstrations.

Laugher, humour and a lightness of spirit have their place in life, especially in the spiritual life. Laughter is a great gift and it's good for the soul as it lifts us up and out of the domination of our circumstances as it relativises our problems.

Prayer: Lord, keep me laughing.

24th Celebration and Joy

This is the day the Lord has made, let us rejoice and be glad in it.
Psalm 118.24.

There are times to mourn and to reflect on what was, but there are also times to celebrate and enjoy the life that we have been given. Humour, laughter and celebration are part of life and it is not a crime to have fun.

Some of the most spiritual people I know are the ones with the keenest sense of humour and their lives are surrounded by laughter.

Religious intensity is a danger in my religious vocation, but thankfully God has a habit of piercing my bubble of over-seriousness with outbreaks of laughter and humour-laden fun.

Prayer: Lord, fill me with your joy and laughter.

25th Giving not Grasping

Being in the form of God, he did not consider equality with God something to be grasped.
Philippians 2.6.

Our Lord did not come into this world to impose his rule or to enforce his rightful position and power.

Instead, he took the form of a servant being born in humble circumstances and voluntarily relinquishing his right to earthly kingship.

He never gave in to the temptation to grab worldly power and impose his rule. Instead, he opened up a new and living way that turned the values and practices of this world on their head.

Prayer: Lord, help me to live as he lived in this world.

26th Life in all its Fullness

I came that they may have life and life in all its fullness.
John 10.10.

The Lord Jesus came to bring life instead of death and freedom instead of bondage. He came to take back what was rightfully his and that possession was us.

We are the sheep of his pasture and the good shepherd risked everything to bring us safely home.

No matter how far we seem to have strayed he is always watching, waiting and searching for us so that he can bring us to the safety of his fold.

With him, there is fullness of life and an abundant supply of joy, peace, laughter, happiness and freedom in his presence.

Prayer: Lord, I joyfully embrace the fullness of life that you came to give me.

27th The Goodness of God

I will make all my goodness pass before you.
Exodus 33.19.

The goodness of God is something that I have become increasingly aware of in my journey of faith.

My experience of the goodness of God has been an ever-expanding reality as he has surprised me with his wonderful goodness on my journey through this world.

God has been outrageously good towards me in my life. His goodness continues to exceed my every expectation.

Prayer: Lord, may your goodness continue to pass before me.

28th Plans to Prosper

I know the plans I have for you, declares the Lord. Plans to prosper you.
Jeremiah 29.11.

Difficult circumstances in life can challenge our faith in God's good intentions toward us. Thankfully, I know deep down that I have God behind me and that he has a good plan for my life, even if I cannot see it.

As I look back over a lifetime of faith in God, I can see how I have been directed and guided by the Lord.

This gives me confidence as I face the future. I trust that God will continue to lead me on his good pathway for my life.

Prayer: Lord, thank you for your plan for my life.

29th No Map

How can we know the way?
John 14.5.

Whilst there is a plan for our lives, we do not possess it.

God has the plan and the map for our future and this means that we are dependent on him to show us the way ahead.

My plans, strategies and preconceived ideas for the future are all contingent as I await God's specific instructions for my life.

What this means in practice is that I am learning to trust God and not myself for my future life.

Prayer: Lord, help me to trust you with my future.

30th Lamentation

By the rivers of Babylon, we sat down and wept, when we remembered Zion.
Psalm 137.1.

There are times when it is important to stop and look back. We need to reflect on the past, where we have been, and what we have done. We may want to weep as we hear songs of lament.

The people who sat weeping by the rivers of Babylon did not stay there, they moved on. They accepted their new situation and began to thrive and prosper in their new home.

Lamentation and its songs have their place, but they are only part of the music of life.

Prayer: Lord, help me to value the past but not to live there.

31st The Best is Yet to Come

Inwardly we are being renewed.
2 Corinthians 4.16.

My faith gives me a present-future perspective rather than a present-past view of this life.

I understand my life to be a journey into God and that I am always moving further forward on this pathway.

Even as my body ages and the wear and tear of life becomes more apparent, I find great joy in the renewing power of God that is at work within me.

Physically the future may hold challenges, but spiritually, I experience daily renewal and growth in my spirit as God leads me onward through my life in this world.

Prayer: Lord, continue to renew my life in you.

Subject Index

A.
Absolute Dependence – August 8th
Absolute Lordship – August 19th
Ambassadors – September 5th
A Beautiful Thing – March 1st
Acting Independently – October 28th
A Different Pressure – March 21st
A Face Full of God – November 18th
A Great Journey – November 27th
A Great Tragedy – August 7th
Alive to God – July 2nd
All My Fountains – July 7th
All Rubbish – November 5th
A Need-To-Know Basis – February 26th
A New Creation – April 5th
A New Heart – March 13th
Apart from Me – August 27th
Apparent Failure – September 24th
Another Comforter – July 8th
A Sabbath Rest – August 24th
A Sense of Wonder – March 7th
A Spiritual Church – June 11th

B.
Back to Life – April 6th
Beginning to See – January 28th
Being Unimportant – October 1st
Being with Him – December 8th
Beyond Ability – May 5th
Beyond Thinking – December 5th
Bondservant – April 15th
Bound Over – October 24th
Breaking – July 17th
Breaking the Mould – June 16th
Bricks Without Straw – September 8th
Building from Within – April 18th

Building on the Rock – November 10th
But Christ – May 13th
By Searching – October 25th

C.

Called to Know – September 7th
Calm Down – January 19th
Carnality – July 21st
Carrying the Presence – August 14th
Celebration and Joy – December 24th
Change – May 3rd
Christ in Everything – August 26th
Christ Lives – February 15th
Close the Door – October 3rd
Co-Crucifixion – November 11th
Collapse – July 29th
Consider Him – November 15th

D.

Day and Night – March 10th
Death – May 10th
Death before Life – November 8th
Deep Change – October 14th
Defilement – September 13th
Desperate Enough – July 5th
Denying Self – August 22nd
Discipline – April 16th
Discovery and Wonder – July 12th
Distracted – August 16th
Divine Power – June 5th
Dogma – October 9th
Doing Nothing – December 18th
Don't Go There – June 18th
Dying to Live – March 18th

E.

Eagles Wings – July 1st
End of Ego – February 14th

Enjoy Life – November 28th
Ever-Increasing – March 3rd
Every Branch – May 16th
Everything is Broken – August 17th
Everything You Have – November 4th
Every Weapon – June 7th
Exactly – September 2nd
Excluding Him – August 15th
Exodus – July 28th
Experiencing God – October 15th

F.
Fading Glory – September 15th
Faithlessness – August 13th
Fear of Tomorrow – April 3rd
Feeling God's Presence – December 14th
Fighting with Fruit – June 8th
Fill All Things – May 24th
Fill Me – September 21st
Filthy Rags – October 16th
Fitting In – September 10th
Flaming Arrows – May 22nd
Focus – May 2nd
Footholds – May 27th
Forty Years – June 13th
Fossilised Remains – March 27th
Freedom – April 24th
From First to Last – September 20th
From the Heart – March 14th

G.
Getting Centred – October 29th
Giving not Grasping – December 25th
Glorious Liberty – March 5th
God Inside – January 4th
God in the Heart – August 5th
God is Active – January 6th
God is Love – December 3rd

God's Own Heart – March 11th
God's Thought – November 3rd
God's Thoughts – May 1st
God's Work – December 12th
Greater Than – May 12th
Grounded in Christ – May 18th
Godly Sorrow – June 23rd
Going Against Myself – April 21st
Guided – September 4th
Guarding My Heart – January 11th

H.

Having Escaped – September 14th
Healing Presence – October 13th
Heart Knowledge – September 26th
Heavenly Mindset – January 12th
Higher Ways – February 27th
His Drum Beat – April 27th
His Healing Presence – October 19th
His Lordship – June 22nd
His Son in Me – February 17th
His Teaching – October 26th
Holding On – October 4th
Human Viewpoints – September 27th
Hunger – September 30th
Hunger and Fullness – August 10th
Hungry Heart – March 9th

I.

I Bow Down – March 6th
I in Him – August 30th
Impartation – July 19th
Imperishable Inheritance – July 25th
Impossible Situations – December 16th
Incorruptible Crowns – July 30th
Increasing Glory – February 5th
Indestructible – November 7th
In Love – May 14th

Intellectual Arrogance – December 17th
Intoxicating – September 19th
It's Your Calling – December 9th
Intuition – June 15th
Internalism not Externalism – June 12th
Inward Longing – May 31st
Inward Renewal – July 3rd
Is This It? – August 4th
I Want to See – January 23rd

J.
Just Thinking – June 20th

K.
Keeping a Safe Distance – June 26th
Know Him – October 18th
Knowing Him – March 2nd
Knowing His Ways – August 1st
Known in Heaven – January 26th

L.
Laughter – December 23rd
Lamentation – December 30th
Learning Christ – October 31st
Let it Go – December 21st
Letting Go – October 5th
Letters from Above – February 22nd
Life in all its Fullness – December 26th
Life to the Body – August 23rd
Like God – August 31st
Living Epistles – January 25th
Living for the Praise – February 28th
Living from Within – February 10th
Living in Him – January 8th
Living in the Centre – June 1st
Living on a Prayer – February 21st
Living out of the New – April 11th
Loosing Sensitivity – July 4th

Lord of My Life – August 3rd
Lord of My Opinions – August 2nd
Lost and Found – December 20th

M.

Manifesting His Presence – March 29th
Many Such Things – August 9th
Ministry of the Spirit – February 24th
More Revelation – August 12th
More than These – October 8th
More will be Given – April 10th
Moved by the Spirit – September 3rd
Moving in the Spirit – September 16th
My House – June 21st
My Soul Gasps – November 9th

N.

Never Perceiving – March 23rd
New for Old – May 20th
New Frontiers in God – August 6th
New Life – April 12th
New Wineskins – April 7th
Next Life – February 16th
No Bypass – April 13th
No House Sharing – July 6th
No Longer Two Lives – April 14th
No Map – December 29th
Non-Conceptual Prayer – December 7th
No One is Righteous – October 10th
Not Conformed – October 9th
Not for Self – September 23rd
Not Found Here – March 25th
Not I But Christ – August 29th
Not One – November 23rd
Not Slow – November 29th
No Settling in Babylon – May 28th

O.

Oblivious – July 27th
On Becoming – February 19th
One in Spirit – April 20th
On Track – July 9th
Our Fight – June 9th
Our Measure – March 20th
Out of My Mind – October 2nd
Out of Egypt – May 29th
Open Doors – December 10th
Opposition – September 25th
Oppression – April 19th

P.
Piggy Backing – July 20th
Plans to Prosper – December 28th
Pleasing Father – August 25th
Personal Sin – December 11th
Positive Faith – May 30th
Possessing Everything – December 2nd
Prayer – December 13th
Pressure – October 21st
Progress Not Perfection – May 9th
Pure Faith – December 6th
Pure Gold – May 8th
Pure in Heart – March 15th

R.
Real Wisdom – March 24th
Reckon Yourself Dead – March 30th
Recognition – August 18th
Recovery of Sight – January 24th
Rejected and Replaced – September 11th
Rejection Hurts – September 12th
Religious Form – June 27th
Relying on God – November 6th
Renewal of My Mind – June 28th
Removing the Veil – January 5th
Resilience – July 16th

Resisters – September 1st
Resting in the Presence – December 19th
Resurrection Ground – June 30th
Resurrection Power – March 28th
Revive Thy Work – August 11th
Ruling and Reigning with Him – July 24th

S.

Saved – September 29th
Sand and Rock – November 17th
Secret and Shameful Ways – June 29th
Seeing Things – January 29th
Seize the Day – April 4th
Self Defence – October 23rd
Self-Denial – March 31st
Self-Improvement – October 17th
Self-Reliance – January 13th
Set Apart from Birth – January 27th
Silence – November 26th
Silence in Heaven – October 20th
Simplicity of Life – November 30th
Small Things – April 28th
So Afraid – January 18th
Soul Force – November 1st
Soul Life – November 2nd
Soul Music – November 14th
Soul Power – February 7th
Soul Rest – November 22nd
Spirit Centred – April 23rd
Spirit Life – February 23rd
Spiritual Ability – April 9th
Spiritual Advance – April 25th
Spiritually Alive – March 16th
Spiritual Awakening – January 1st
Spiritual Birth – February 9th
Spiritual Capacities – June 3rd
Spiritual Not Religious – January 14th
Spiritual Enlargement – January 20th

Spiritual Faculties – July 10th
Spiritual Food – February 12th
Spiritual Formation – January 16th
Spiritual Ground – June 2nd
Spiritual Growth – February 8th
Spiritual Healing – December 1st
Spiritual Increase – March 8th
Spiritual Illumination – January 3rd
Spiritual Maturity – January 17th
Spiritual Intelligence – February 29th
Spiritual Possessiveness – October 12th
Spiritual Thirst – January 7th
Spiritual Transformation – January 2nd
Strengthen what Remains – May 6th
Stumble and Fall – November 19th
Suffering Many Things – February 13th
Supernatural Battle – July 11th
Surrender All – April 22nd
Surrender – January 30th

T.

Tarry – August 28th
Taken Captive – June 17th
The Abolition of 'I' – May 11th
The Adventure – July 13th
The Best is Yet to Come – December 31st
The Communion of Saints – June 19th
The Counsel of God – January 31st
The Cares of this World – December 15th
The Crucified Life – April 26th
The Desires – September 18th
The Despised Things – June 25th
The Dictatorship of Ego – May 26th
The Difference – June 10th
The Divine Builder – April 17th
The Eternal Purpose of God – July 26th
The Fashion of this World – April 2nd
The Firstborn – March 19th

The Fullness of God – February 2nd
The Gardner – May 15th
The God Who Speaks – August 20th
The Goodness of God – December 27th
The Great Exception – February 3rd
The Hearts Dialogue – October 6th
The Kiss of Life – March 17th
The Lamp of the Lord – November 12th
The Lord's Discipline – April 30th
The Manifestation of Christ – September 6th
The Meditation of My Heart – September 28th
The Mystery – March 4th
The Outer Appearance – October 27th
The Prime Mover – April 8th
The Promised Land – February 1st
The Quest – July 14th
The Rest Laboratory – July 18th
The River – March 12th
The Sacred Gaze – February 6th
The Sanctuary – November 24th
The Source – July 31st
The Spirit of Life – January 22nd
The Truth – November 13th
The Way Back to God – January 9th
The Weakness of God – March 22nd
The Whole Measure – May 19th
The Witness – November 16th
The Will of Father – June 24th
The Worship of the Heart – February 4th
Things Above – May 4th
This Foundation – May 17th
This is That – July 15th
Tomorrows World – February 11th
Total Dependence – October 7th
Transcendent Union – October 11th
Trouble – October 22nd
Training for War – June 6th
True Freedom – December 22nd

Trusting God – January 10th
Trusting the Lord – April 29th
Trusting the Plan – January 15th

U.
Unholy Trinity – May 21st
Upgraded in God – February 18th

V.
Visible or Invisible – June 14th

W.
Wait – May 23rd
Waiting on the Lord – November 21st
Waiting Patiently – October 30th
Waiting with God – March 26th
Wash Me – May 25th
Watch – December 4th
Weaned off the World – June 4th
We Have Fellowship – September 17th
What God Has Prepared – July 22nd
What I am Here For – July 23rd
When All Is Stripped Away – November 25th
Who Am I – February 20th
Who Stopped You? – September 22nd
Without Holiness – August 21st
Without Me – November 20th
Wisdom Among the Mature – February 25th

Y.
Your Affections – May 7th
Your Ways – April 1st
Your Will – January 21st